Safe, Sound and Secure

How to Protect Your
•Identity •Privacy •Money •Computers •Cellphones
•Car •Home •Email
•Internet Use •Wireless Networks
•Credit, Debit and ATM cards •Financial Accounts

Don Silver

Adams-Hall Publishing
Los Angeles

Library of Congress Cataloging-in-Publication Data

Silver, Don- author.
Title: Safe, sound and secure : how to protect your identity, privacy, money, computers, cellphones, car, home, email, internet use, wireless networks, credit, debit and ATM cards, financial accounts / Don Silver.
Description: Los Angeles : Adams-Hall Publishing, [2016]
Identifiers: LCCN 2016005116
ISBN 9780944708675 (print book) | ISBN 9780944708684 (e-book)
Subjects: LCSH: Computer networks—Security measures-Popular works. | Computer security—Popular works. | Identity theft—Prevention—Popular works. | Personal information management—Popular works. | Disclosure of information—Popular works.
Classification: LCC TK5105.59 .S555 2016 | DDC 005.8—dc23
LC record available at https://lccn.loc.gov/201600511

PRAISE FOR DON SILVER'S TEACH YOUR COMPUTER TO DANCE

"You can pick any page at random and find yourself saying, 'That's a good idea.'"
—Andrew Kantor, Technology Columnist, *USA TODAY*

"I learned something new on almost every page. This book is crammed full of valuable hints and tips."
—Andrew Blackman, Reporter, *The Wall Street Journal*

"I like this book a lot. It's written by people who know what they're talking about and who are up on the latest PC and Internet technologies—and who are able to offer direct advice to those who are ready for technological adventure."
—Jonathan Zittrain, Professor of Internet Governance and Regulation, *Oxford University* and Co-Founder of *Harvard Law School's Berkman Center for Internet & Society*

"Has dozens of expert tips for securing your computing experience. It also contains a ton of great advice for readers of any level."
—Roger A. Grimes, Security Adviser Columnist, *InfoWorld* and author of four books on Windows computer security including *Professional Windows Desktop and Server Hardening*

"A great resource for anyone who spends time online. This is a terrific resource on how to get the *most* out of your computer and online experience and at the same time practice 'safe computing.'"
—Fran Maier, Executive Director and President, *TRUSTe*

"Highly recommended for *all* computer users… is full of practical tips and sound advice presented in an easy-to- read format."
—Suzi Turner, Spyware researcher and consultant, owner of *SpywareWarrior.com* and writer of the *Spyware Confidential* blog, ZDNet.com

Table of Contents

Read This First

Even the late George Orwell, the author of *1984*, would be surprised by the invasion of privacy and lack of security we face today. He would be even more surprised by the type and volume of information people give up *voluntarily*.

Now, more than ever, you need to do the best you can to protect yourself while you're awake as well as when you're sleeping. Read this book and you'll understand the best steps (not every step) you can take to protect yourself.

Getting more security and privacy is always a tradeoff

The tradeoff with security and privacy is comparing what you're getting with what you're giving up. While no privacy and security measures are perfect, taking the right steps will help you avoid the missteps and mistakes that can cost you financially, medically and emotionally.

There are two parts to today's security and privacy—the information you voluntarily give up and what is taken from you behind your back or in front of your face.

Keep in mind that in our high-tech society, part of that security/privacy tradeoff is that there is no free lunch. You aren't really getting free searches, free email, free social media, etc. The true cost for these "free services" is that information about you is being gathered and used for marketing and other purposes.

How easy is it to identify people by the traces they leave?

In one experiment, researchers could identify purchasers 90% of the time by looking at just three credit-card transactions if the prices of the items purchased were included—this is *without* even seeing the names, addresses, email addresses or other personal information of the cardholders. When the price information was removed, it took only four transactions to identify people.

Your Internet connection may be vulnerable

When the Internet is involved, the opportunity for hacking is always there especially if you don't take protective steps. The risk is present not only for your computer, tablet or phone but also for cars, TVs, tea kettles, baby monitors, thermometers, pregnancy tests, lightbulbs, thermostats, household appliances and even toilets if they are connected to or can be accessed by the Internet.

Believe it or not, a Japanese toilet was hacked remotely—the toilet lid seemed to have a mind of its own as it raised and lowered!

Your smart TV with a built-in webcam for video chatting and voice recognition may be vulnerable, too.

Previously, the best way to secure a device was to unplug it. Now with wireless and rechargeable devices always on, that solution is no longer always viable.

Many people think that mobile devices are always secure, unaware that there are hundreds of thousands of unique malware programs designed just for such devices.

What's at risk?

To avoid security and privacy disasters, you need to *proactively* protect and secure yourself, your children and other loved ones; your home and work environment; your car, computers and mobile devices; and your financial, social-networking and medical information.

Probably the worst kind of identity theft is medical identity theft. It can affect not only your finances but also your medical record. On the black market, your medical information is worth roughly ten times more than any of your credit-card numbers.

The good news

Fortunately, there are strategies and techniques to help prevent or remedy attacks on you, your computer, your mobile devices, your information and your identity—both on and off the Internet.

How this book is organized

The table of contents and index list the topics covered in the book. You can either read the book from beginning to end or just zero in on particular topics of interest. There is some intentional repetition of important information as needed, along with a few pertinent cross references.

In this book, the word "computer" generally refers to tablets, too, and in some cases phones as well.

The goal of this book is to help you sleep better at night and function more safely and privately 24/7.

1. Identity Theft—Preventing and Fixing

Dealing With the 9 Types of Identity Theft

There's a lot to know about identity theft including:

- How identity theft occurs
- How to spot the nine types of identity theft
- How to prevent identity theft
- How to handle identity theft if it occurs

When most people think of identity theft, they just think of someone using someone else's credit cards or stealing money from a bank account. There's much more to it.

You may discover identity theft has occurred when your doctor asks you about medical treatment you haven't received; you get turned down for a job, a rental or utility services; you start getting mail in someone else's name; your bank and other financial statements stop arriving in the mail; you can't get credit for a car or a mortgage; you can't open a bank account; or you can't get social services.

Internet identity theft is always morphing. Now Internet malware is designed not for mischief but rather to steal your money, your data and maybe your identity.

Nine main types of identity theft

1. Financial Identity Theft

With financial identity theft, a thief takes over your existing assets or creates a new identity in your name or with your identifying number, which costs you money and/or causes you trouble.

Types of financial identity theft

There are many types of financial identity theft including:

- Opening new accounts in your name

- Completely taking over existing accounts or withdrawing money from them

  A bounced check could result and depending on your state, that could lead to an arrest warrant being issued in your name.

- "Washing" checks to change the payee and amount

- Duplicating your checks

- Recording fraudulent mortgages and property deeds

  Consequently, it's a good idea to check real estate records from time to time.

- Getting medical care with your health insurance policy or running up medical bills in your name

- Listing your car insurance policy when the thief has an accident

- Using your business license, professional license or fictitious business name

- Business takeover fraud

  With this type of fraud, businesses are tricked into transferring money into fraudulent bank accounts by using publicly available information and weaknesses in a business's email system.

Hackers get access to email passwords to send false wire transfer instructions on legitimate purchases. So the purchase is real but the payee is the hacker's account.

If you have a small business, you may be targeted because you may not have the money or expertise to secure your business.

Get needed insurance for your business.

Chapter 2 has more information on preventing financial identity theft.

2. Medical Identity Theft

Medical identity theft affects millions of people each year. This can sometimes be more difficult to clean up and more costly than financial identity theft alone. Both types of identity theft can occur from the same theft because medical files often also contain Social Security numbers, birth dates and credit-card information.

Medical and financial problems

With medical identity theft, someone else's blood type, test results, medications, allergies and other medical conditions may be mixed in with your medical records.

This could prove to be inconvenient or fatal.

What can make this more difficult to clean up is that federal medical-privacy laws prevent you from seeing someone else's information even if it's in your medical file.

And to add financial insult to injury, unlike the limits on credit-card fraud that may be available, there are no monetary limits on losses with these erroneous medical bills if you can't prove your innocence.

Your credit report and medical bills

When you check your *financial* credit reports each year (or more often), see whether there are any unpaid medical bills on there that could hurt your credit and affect your ability to get jobs, buy or rent a place or get insurance.

Your form of payment may expose your medical information

Your health information may become part of a financial records database when you pay by credit or debit card for medical services or prescriptions.

Unpaid medical bills can contain your information

You may inadvertently spread information about your medical care because unpaid medical bills can become part of your credit file at the financial credit bureaus. If the name of the medical provider is on the reports, it may indicate the type of medical treatment you received.

Your doctor's office

When you see a doctor or other medical provider for the first time, you are usually given an intake sheet to list your medical history along with your date of birth, Social Security number and driver's license number (and maybe that of family members).

Many years ago, I experienced identity theft and was able to trace it to a doctor's intake form. Since then, I no longer provide my Social Security number or driver's license number on these forms. I tell the doctors' offices about my identity-theft experience and I haven't encountered any resistance from doctors' offices when I omit this sensitive information.

Of course, there are times when you do need to disclosure your Social Security number to get medical care such as with Medicare and Medicaid. Some health-insurance companies also require the number.

Who else can see your medical records?

Health, life and disability insurance companies have access to your medical records as may government agencies such as the Centers for Medicare & Medicaid Services, Social Security Disability and Workers Compensation agencies.

In addition, agencies of the federal government may issue administrative subpoenas (without prior judicial approval) to gain access to medical records.

And, as electronic health records (EHR) become common, so do the risks for loss of privacy on these records because of security breaches.

HIPAA

Your first line of defense in protecting your medical information is HIPAA (the Health Insurance Portability and Accountability Act).

This federal law can help protect information about the physical or mental health, treatments you've received and payment information for healthcare services. States can and may enact stronger privacy laws.

You can correct errors in your health records under HIPAA. This could be especially important if someone impersonates you and gets medical care in your name.

Not everything is covered by HIPAA. Employment or school records may include medical information. School records are under another federal law, FERPA (Family Education Rights and Privacy Act). And at work, ask whether employee-wellness program information and any work-sponsored genetic-testing results become part of your personnel file.

Medical apps

Think twice before you use an app that makes your medical records available on your cellphone. At this time, health records on an app are not protected by HIPAA. As a result, your medical records could be shared or sold by the app developer.

Health and fitness apps

To be effective, mobile health and fitness apps need certain information about you. However, the apps may ask for more than what may be needed for the app to work. Such extra information may include your name, age, gender, height, weight, exercise routine, menstrual cycle and pregnancy status.

The mobile app may not be secure. You may be submitting this information unencrypted to a less-than-secure website (an https website is more secure than an http website). Even if your information arrives securely at the app company, it may not be stored securely at the app's website or on its servers.

Your data may then be transmitted over unsecured Internet connections to data brokers or advertisers who would have information on your diseases and conditions.

Also, a hacker nearby may use Bluetooth to hack your device.

See if the privacy settings on the app can be adjusted for more privacy.

If you stop using the app, see if you can delete your information both at the company and on your device.

Your prescriptions and Pharmacy Benefit Managers

As for your prescriptions, Pharmacy Benefit Managers (PBMs) have your prescription history through health plans. Keep track of your own prescription history so you can catch errors.

To protect your prescription-history privacy:

- See whether your doctor participates in the American Medical Association's Physician Data Restriction Program (PDRP). Doctors can opt out of having prescription information used for pharmaceutical marketing purposes. Even with an opt-out, AMA can still have information from the "Physician Masterfile."

- Pay prescription bills on time so the bills don't find their way into your financial credit report.

If you decide to participate in a pharmaceutical company prescription-financial-assistance program to hold down your costs, read the fine print. In return for the discounted price, you may be agreeing to allow the company access to (and the ability to sell) part or all of your current and past medical history and information.

Your prescription reports

You can get a copy of your prescription history by contacting Milliman, http://www.rxhistories.com/RequestAReport/

Of course, law enforcement and the court system may have access, too, to perform their jobs.

Your non-prescription information

You may purchase non-prescription products to help with your medical conditions. If you use a credit or debit card or become part of a store's database through a valued-customer program, you are creating another trail for someone to know the health details of your life.

Information you volunteer

In addition, you may end up voluntarily providing medical information on yourself through fitness and health apps; social-networking websites; online chats; Internet searches on diseases, illnesses and products; and information you provide when you apply for an insurance policy.

If you participate in online chats or medical forums, you may want to use a pseudonym to keep your privacy.

You may inadvertently provide medical information on yourself by the websites you visit because cookies on your device track and help identify you. You may have no control over how all this information is used.

As medical treatment via the Internet becomes more common, it carries with it the risk that the privacy of your medical data will be breached during transmission and storage.

Medical-information and medical-alert devices

As with other medical alternatives, these devices provide medical information on you. How securely is it stored? How secure is the transmission of your data? Is your information shared with any company?

PHR (Personal Health Records)

PHRs allow you to manage and store your health information including your medical history, conditions, test results, prescriptions and treatment plans. As with anything stored at another location, there is a risk of having a privacy breach or being subject to a court order to reveal your records.

Hospitals and medical devices

Because many medical devices are networked and connected to the Internet, they can be controlled (and hacked) remotely. Such devices include infusion pumps that deliver medication, pacemakers and many others. Greater security efforts are needed for medical devices.

3. Income-Tax Identity Theft

Identity theft can affect your income-tax returns and refunds.

This is not a rare event. The IRS has already given or offered special ID numbers to more than three million households that have experienced actual or potential income-tax identity theft.

It can take years to resolve identity-theft issues with the IRS and state authorities and get any refund due to you. You may also be dealing with law enforcement agency affidavits as well as repairing and monitoring your credit for years.

How income-tax identity theft can affect you

An identity thief can use your Social Security number to file a false income-tax return, claim a refund and have the refund sent to the thief's address. Or a thief might just steal your return when you mail it or steal a refund check out of your mail box.

Another way you could be affected is where a thief gets a job and uses your Social Security number to report income. Then when you file your income-tax return, it appears to the IRS that you haven't reported all of your income.

Steps you can take to prevent it

Be sure to have a strong password if you file your tax return online. Always do a virus scan and a spyware scan before preparing your tax returns and filing them online.

Also, save the data and return on a flash or separate backup drive not connected to the Internet (for more security) rather than on your computer and print out a copy of your return for your records. If the information is ever on your computer and you just delete it in the recycling or trash bin, that information may still be obtainable if your computer gets hacked.

Make sure your paper records and files are secure, too. Use a cross-cut (or better yet, a micro-cut) shredder to shred any tax-related papers you no longer need.

Before you select a tax preparer, ask whether they use encryption and what computer-security software they use. See whether they leave out papers for other clients on their desks that could compromise you if those papers were yours. Find out how long the preparer has been in the tax-preparation business.

Adjust your withholding to minimize the size of future tax refunds that could be taken by identity thieves.

What to do if tax-identity theft happens

If this happens to you, get legal and tax advice and notify the IRS and your state (and local) taxing authority. Consider getting an IRS Identity Protection (IP) PIN at https://www.irs.gov/Individuals/Get-An-Identity-Protection-PIN

The IRS Identity Protection Specialized Unit is at 1.800.908.4490.

Also see the IRS Identity Theft Affidavit at

https://www.irs.gov/pub/irs-pdf/f14039.pdf

States should have their own identity-theft affidavit form.

Note that the IRS uses the mail, not email or a phone call, to contact taxpayers. If you get an email or phone calls from someone claiming to be from the IRS, contact the IRS with the form at:
https://www.treasury.gov/tigta/contact_report_scam.shtml

Note that some taxpayers have found that their IP PINs have been stolen.

4. Employment Identity Theft

As noted above, if someone works under your name or uses your Social Security number, the IRS will ask why you aren't reporting all of your income and paying all of your taxes. There have also been cases where someone impersonates another person to use their state-issued license to conduct business.

One way to spot problems is to periodically review your credit reports from the three credit-reporting agencies (Equifax, Experian and TransUnion) and see what they show regarding your work history (including your occupation and location of work). You can also look at your Social Security earnings record at: https://www.ssa.gov

5. Governmental Identity Theft

An identity thief has a lot of choices when it comes to stealing your identity on the federal, state and/or local governmental levels—choices that include going after the following:

- Social Security
- Medicare

- Medicaid
- Veterans' benefits
- Unemployment benefits
- Welfare benefits
- EBT (food-stamp benefits)
- Income-tax refunds
- Student loans
- Driver's license
- Bankruptcies (filed in your name)
- Child-support notices (where you're listed as the parent and you really aren't).

To prevent Social Security issues, take a look each year at your free Social Security Statement (go to https://www.ssa.gov/myaccount/). You can also call the general Social Security Administration number at 1.800.772.1213 or the Social Security fraud number at 1.800.269.0271.

If you need to file your own bankruptcy, ask your attorney about not accidentally listing any fraudulently opened accounts in your bankruptcy (which could cause you to be responsible for them).

For student-loan fraud issues, you can call 1.800.647.8733 to contact the U.S. Department of Education Office of Inspector General Hotline.

6. Criminal Identity Theft

Just when you thought it couldn't get any worse, now you get to read about criminal identity theft.

If someone is stopped for a traffic ticket or arrested, they may give your name or personally identifiable information (e.g., your Social Security number, date of birth, driver's license number, etc.) instead of their own to law enforcement. You may be unaware of this until you're turned down for a job or your employment is terminated.

If you suffer criminal identity theft, get legal advice on clearing your name and doing the following:

- Contacting the arresting law enforcement agency as well as other governmental agencies such as Social Security, the IRS, the Secretary of State (for passports) and the Department of Motor Vehicles so they are made aware of the criminal identity theft through a false-impersonation identity-theft report.

- Arranging for an impersonation investigation that results in a declaration of your innocence as well as revised records that show the imposter's name, not yours.

- Getting written documentation (e.g., a letter of clearance from a court) that you can keep on your person showing you are an innocent victim of identity theft and not the imposter. Unfortunately, you may need to carry this letter with you forever.

  If a court is involved in your case, request that the court issue an order that the imposter is forbidden to have any information on you and that all of your information (whether hard copy, in the cloud or on a computer drive or other electronic device) in the possession of the imposter is returned to you.

- Making sure background investigating companies and credit reporting agencies correct their records.

7. Child, Student and College Identity Theft

Thieves like to target children for identity theft because there's a greater chance it can take longer (sometimes years) for this type of theft to be discovered—children aren't checking their credit reports.

If your child has a Social Security number, identity thieves may use it for years without your knowledge to get loans, credit cards and financial accounts, apply for government benefits and more.

Prevention is the best cure

Restrict who has your child's information.

Be aware that child identity theft may involve relatives or friends.

Your child's school may put out a print or online directory that includes students' information and is available to the general public. If so, make sure you look for and respond to opt-out notices. Under federal law, you have approval rights regarding the disclosure of your child's personal information – www2.ed.gov/policy/gen/guid/fpco/ferpa/index.html

Schools may also do surveys that collect information on the children. You have the right to see materials before they are given to students (see http://familypolicy.ed.gov/).

Protecting you from your children

Although you need to protect your children while they are on the Internet, you also need to protect yourself from your children if your children:

- Have access to your computer, tablet or phone
- Know your passwords

- Use your administrator mode (see Chapter 5) on your computer (and not a separate, limited mode) where they have access to sensitive areas of your device that should only be accessed by you

Protecting your children with COPPA

The COPPA Rule (Children's Online Privacy Protection Act) was put in place to protect children's personal information on websites and online services—including apps—that are directed to children under 13.

COPPA requires those sites and services to notify parents directly and get their approval before they collect, use, or disclose a child's personal information.

Personal information for COPPA includes a child's name, address, phone number or email address; their physical whereabouts; photos, videos and audio recordings of the child, and persistent identifiers, like IP addresses, that can be used to track a child's activities over time and across different websites and online services.

Before your child uses features on a site or downloads an app that collects their personal information, you should get a plain language notice about what information the site will collect, how it will use it, and how you can provide your consent.

If you think a site has collected information from your kids or marketed to them in a way that violates the law, you can report it to the FTC at https://www.ftccomplaintassistant.gov/#crnt&panel1-1

Right time to get a child's credit report

Before your child applies for college, financial aid or a job or rents an apartment, get a credit report so there is enough time to correct any errors.

Contact all three of the following credit-reporting agencies:

- Equifax www.equifax.com
- Experian www.experian.com
- TransUnion www.transunion.com

How to check whether child identity theft has occurred

The first step is to find out if a credit report exists on your child. If you choose to do this, have the search done on the child's Social Security number since a thief might use another name, address and birth date.

Warning: Keep in mind that you may be creating a problem where one doesn't exist because your inquiry on a non-existent credit report may cause one to be created (which an identity thief can later access).

What you want to find out is that there is *no* credit report on file—that decreases the chances that identity fraud is going on.

If a report does exist, consider placing a credit (security) freeze on your child's reports by contacting the three credit-reporting agencies (Equifax, Experian and TransUnion) to prevent future credit and financial transactions. Note, however, not all states allow a parent or guardian to place a credit freeze on a minor's credit report.

Get legal advice about contacting the police and the businesses involved and filing a Federal Trade Commission fraud report. See https://www.ftccomplaintassistant.gov/

Also see https://www.identitytheft.gov/#what-to-do-right-away

When your children start school

When your child starts school, whether it's preschool or kindergarten, your child's information is being collected. That information may include the student's name, address, date of birth, place of birth, Social Security number, mother's maiden name, fingerprints, retina patterns, DNA and more. Ask who will have access to the information and read the privacy policies.

See if your child can opt out of information collection so it doesn't end up in a directory or military recruitment list. There are laws on the federal and state level to protect students' information. The federal law is FERPA (the Family Educational Rights and Privacy Act also known as the Buckley Amendment). (Homeschoolers are not protected by FERPA but some states have enacted protective laws for them.)

When your children are in college

Parents may be surprised to learn that they generally *don't* have access to information on their child's college status.

Under FERPA, you as a parent basically have no rights to know how your children are doing in school once they are at least 18 years old or enrolled at a postsecondary institution.

Generally, even if you as a parent are paying all of the tuition, you have no right to know your child's grades or mental-health status *unless* your student child gives permission. In some cases, a waiver for the parent's access to information may be given and colleges can alert you to drug or alcohol problems and sexual offenses.

College students face the same security issues as the general population but they should pay special attention to the following:

- Be careful when using hotspots or public computers (e.g., at libraries) to access your information in the cloud.

- Don't loan your driver's license or other identification card.

- Use a college credit card with a low limit rather than a debit card to minimize liability for erroneous or fraudulent charges.

- Be very careful in sharing files or access to your devices including peer-to-peer file sharing programs.

- Don't leave your computer or other devices unattended where mischief or worse can be done by others.

- Minimize posting sensitive personal information on social-networking sites.
  Some colleges are developing apps that improve campus safety by connecting directly to national emergency hotlines or campus-security offices or using a Bluetooth panic button.

Other apps offer virtual escorts that monitor students traveling across campus at night or send messages with GPS coordinates if someone is overdue at a location.

8. Senior Identity Theft

In general, it is easier for criminals to fool seniors to obtain financial and personal information whether it's over the phone, by email, in person or by mail. And the identity theft may go undetected for a long period of time if seniors don't keep track of their financial affairs.

The risk is that bank accounts can be emptied, credit cards can be used without authorization, loans can be taken out in the name of a senior or seniors can be tricked into signing wills, trusts, powers of attorney or contracts.

Seniors should ***not***:

- Give caregivers access to personal and financial information
- Carry their Medicare card and/or Social Security card (or number) in their wallet or purse unless absolutely needed that day
- Respond to scam phone calls with callers posing as banks, charities, insurance companies or the government
- Click on malware links in emails or on links at false websites
- Inadvertently participate in Medicare fraud by getting "free" medical equipment

9. Deceased Identity Theft

Wow, your identity can be stolen even after you die.

Loved ones should be careful about the details they put in an obituary notice. They could be providing your birth date, birth place, work history and family-tree information (including a mother's maiden name). Maybe it's better to just list the birth and death years rather than exact dates.

There are two areas of concern with deceased persons.

First, it is possible to steal the identity of deceased persons. The necessary information can be available from obituaries and websites that have the Social Security Death Index (to assist with genealogy efforts).

Although the Social Security Administration contacts credit bureaus on deaths, it takes time to do this. When a loved one passes away, it's a good idea to do the following: (1) contact the credit reporting agencies (Equifax, Experian and TransUnion) in writing (by certified mail, return receipt requested) to advise them of the death; (2) request that they not issue any more credit; (3) place an alert on the credit file; and (4) if someone tries to get credit in the deceased's name, to notify the appropriate person (e.g., the executor, trustee, etc.). Of course, keep a copy of all your correspondence.

It's also a good idea to promptly contact credit-card companies, banks, other financial institutions and mortgage companies to let them know about the death.

To remove a deceased relative from commercial marketing lists, go to https://www.ims-dm.com/cgi/ddnc.php

The second area of concern is where no one knows the passwords or security question answers of the deceased person. It can become very difficult to get access to needed information after a death.

Possible solutions are sharing this information with a close, trusted relative or friend while you're alive or keeping a copy in your safe deposit box to be accessed if you die or become incapacitated. Consult with your attorney on the best approach for you and how your estate-planning documents may need to deal with this issue.

*****

Social Security Numbers

Your Social Security number (SSN) is the most powerful piece of information an identity thief wants. With it, the thief can:

- Establish credit in your name including mortgages and student loans
- File tax returns and maybe get your tax refunds
- Open accounts and possibly access your financial and credit-card accounts
- Maybe get medical care in your name (this can be especially dangerous for you since someone else's medical information, prescriptions and treatments can be confused with yours)
- Get governmental benefits in your name such as unemployment, Medicaid, Social Security and food stamps
- Get a driver's license

Protecting your SSN

Don't print your SSN on checks or other documents. Don't use any part of your SSN as your ATM or other pin number. Before you share your SSN with anyone, ask why they need it, how they'll protect it and what the consequences are if you don't provide it. Try to leave that space on a form blank, see if another identifying document can be used or if necessary, just list the last four digits of your SSN.

Don't carry your SSN or card in your wallet or purse. Only take your Medicare card (which has your SSN) outside your home when necessary. Don't carry your passport or birth certificate either unless absolutely necessary.

In a public place, including at a bank where you may need to provide your SSN, whisper your SSN or better yet, write it down so no one overhears it.

Consider getting a credit (security) freeze to prevent misuse of your Social Security number.

Get your free credit reports each year from Equifax, Experian and TransUnion and check them over to see if new credit or mortgage accounts have been established in your name without your knowledge.

You can block access to your Social Security record (and SSN) at https://secure.ssa.gov/acu/IPS_INTR/blockaccess

For extra security, you can require a cellphone text message code for signing in to your record at Social Security.

Check your Social Security online statement of earnings and also work history (Form 7050) from yearly to make sure no one else is using your SSN.

If you need to change your SSN

In an extreme case, the Social Security Administration (SSA) may change your Social Security number.

Ask for a letter from SSA explaining they have issued you a new SSN. This letter should state you will no longer be using the old number and only the new number will be valid. This letter is important when changing over personal, pertinent documents (e.g., transcripts) and/or accounts (e.g., bank accounts) to the newly issued number.

Check your work history (Form 7050) from the SSA. Have a corrected work history transferred from your old SSN file to your new SSN file.

Note that your Social Security number won't be erased from the Social Security system.

Have the SSA flag your old file and note that anyone using the old number is an imposter.

Even with the change, in some records your new number will still be tied to your old number to provide continuity. Also, it's not automatic that all relevant governmental agencies and businesses will know about the new number. You may have a lot of legwork to do to get everyone up to speed.

A new number doesn't solve all of your problems and it may create new ones. For example, since you won't have a credit history under the new Social Security number, you may have a more difficult time getting a job, applying for home credit, making a car purchase, renting an apartment, getting insurance or opening a bank account. See Identity Theft and Your Social Security Number at: http://www.ssa.gov/pubs/EN-05-10064.pdf

*****

Medicare Numbers

If you need to bring your Medicare card (which has your Social Security number on it) to a doctor's office, just carry it with you for that day.

*****

Other Tips for Preventing or Minimizing Identity Theft

- Before you share your information at a doctor's office, business, school or workplace, always first ask why the information is needed and how it will be safeguarded.

Be particularly cautious when asked for your Social Security number, your driver's license number, your mother's maiden name or your birthdate, especially all of these at once. Just because a form asks for confidential, sensitive information doesn't always mean you have to provide it. Express your concern about identity theft if you decide not to provide all the requested information.

These pieces of your identity are most often used to prove who you say you are when conducting financial and other important transactions over the phone, through the mail or via the Internet.

When filling out forms or responding to requests for information, try to avoid giving out these pieces of information. If you must disclose your information, see if one or two of these items are enough or you can supply less (e.g., having just the last four digits of your Social Security number rather than the entire number).

- Don't believe callers who say they're from your credit-card company or bank calling to prevent fraud on your account. Instead, look at your own records (e.g., credit-card statement or the back of a credit card) or check on the Internet for the phone number to call. Don't immediately believe that whoever is contacting you is really from your company and is giving you a real call-back phone number for the company.

- Set up fraud alerts or probably better yet, credit (security) freezes, with the three credit-reporting agencies (Equifax, Experian and TransUnion).

- Consider setting up alerts for financial and credit-card accounts so you know all the transactions happening in your accounts via text or email.

- Report any suspicious activity immediately to the relevant institution so that you can try to minimize any damage.

- Be very careful when giving out personal or financial information on the phone and over the Internet.

- Avoid clicking on links in emails.

- Don't open an email with an unusual subject line even if it's from someone you know—instead, call the sender to confirm whether the person sent it or malware did.

- Don't send money or deposit a check (and send some of the check proceeds back) in response to an email or letter to get a job, obtain a prize, collect foreign lottery winnings or participate in any deal that sounds too good to be true.

- Check your credit reports regularly for accounts you didn't set up as well as for balances that don't match up with your records (you can space out the free, annual credit reports from Equifax, Experian and TransUnion so you receive one every four months).

- Get advice on how long to keep each type of document. When documents are ready to be discarded, shred them. Such documents include income-tax returns, expired charge cards, receipts, credit-card offers, credit applications, insurance forms, physician statements, medical records, checks and bank and other financial statements.

  Be sure to shred unneeded documents with at least a cross-cut/confetti-cut shredder or incinerate (if allowed in your municipality) them so they can't be put back together by an identity thief. A cross-cut (or better yet, a micro-cut) shredder that cuts paper and credit cards gives you more privacy than straight-cut shredders. There are commercial services, too, that handle shredding.

You have paper and electronic records. Some records are very important to an identity thief such as your Social Security card and birth certificate.

Your important paper records should probably be kept in a safe deposit box.

- Your electronic records should be encrypted. Files should be backed up regularly. Be aware that you have less control over records that are stored in the cloud.

  For records on your computer's hard disk, flash drives or other devices that you no longer need, you should not only use specialized software to remove the data on the devices, it's probably also a good idea to have the devices physically destroyed, too.

  For records in the cloud, the data's destruction depends on the terms of service with the cloud provider.

- Pay attention to your medical benefit statements to look for charges from medical providers you didn't see.

- Have strong, complex passwords and different passwords for each website or service whether at work or at home.

- Don't give anyone your passwords whether at work or at home.

- Use the highest level of privacy settings on websites and services.

- Before signing up for an app or a service, see what information it wants from you and who has access to it.

- File your income taxes well before April 15 to beat the imposter and help prevent someone else from filing a false return and claiming a refund in your name.

- You need to be careful at home and work and being out in public.

  At home, don't make it easy for visitors to access your information or passwords. Lock up your financial documents and records in a safe place at home and likewise for your purse or wallet at work.

- Middle names—Although not using your middle initial or middle name can give you more privacy, the risk is that you may get confused with people who have similar names in databases, resulting in other people with your name (but not your middle name or middle initial) getting access to your information from certain companies or websites.

- Trusts—Ask your attorney about more private ways to name your trust so it's not too easy to track ownership of assets to you and to reveal what kind of trust you've set up.

- On warranty registration cards, just provide your contact information (e.g., don't list income, age and other personal information).

- You may create a website but not want people to discover your name and address. Generally, this information is public information unless you make it private by requesting private registration. There is a proposal to eliminate private (anonymous) domain registration.

- In many cases, political campaigns assemble extremely detailed information about voters for targeted advertisements, door-to-door canvassing and phone calls. These political dossiers may be the largest amount of unregulated personal data. The large accumulation and cross-referencing of this data makes it an inviting target for hackers.

  When you register to vote, you may have a choice as to listing your email address and phone number. Note that if you do list your information, the amount of political and other phone calls and email may become burdensome and you will have provided information that may also be used by an identity thief.

*****

Fraud Alerts

Note: A "fraud alert" is *not* the same as a credit (security) freeze. A credit (security) freeze is more powerful in protecting your credit but it may not be the right choice for you (*see* Credit Freezes below).

To help prevent identity fraud, you can keep placing a no-cost, 90-day *fraud alert* that covers the three credit-reporting agencies (Equifax, Experian and TransUnion). When you place an alert with one of the three agencies, that agency notifies the other two. (With *credit freezes*, you *do* need to contact each of the three agencies.)

You can renew the alert over and over again every 90 days.

With an alert in place, you are *supposed to be* contacted before new credit (e.g., a new credit card) is authorized but that doesn't always happen. That's another reason you should monitor your credit reports and possibly have a more powerful credit (security) freeze, instead of a fraud alert, in effect.

If you're in the military or you're a victim of identity theft, you may be able to get a longer fraud alert.

If you're on active duty and don't want to place a credit freeze on your credit-agency reporting accounts, you can place an active-duty fraud alert that lasts a year instead of the usual 90-day period. You can also appoint someone as your representative if you are outside the U.S.

With a police report showing identity theft, you can get a seven-year fraud alert and you may be able to add a statement as to any information you have about the fraud.

If you file a fraud alert, you are entitled to free copies of your credit report from the three credit-reporting agencies in addition to your free once-a-year reports.

- Equifax: https://www.alerts.equifax.com/AutoFraud_Online/jsp/fraudAlert.jsp

- Experian: https://www.experian.com/fraud/center.html

- TransUnion: https://www.transunion.com/fraud-victim-resource/place-fraud-alert

*****

Credit Freezes (Security Freezes)

A credit (security) freeze is much more powerful than a fraud alert. To prevent other people from taking out new loans or getting new credit in your name, put a credit/security freeze on your accounts with the three credit-reporting agencies (Equifax, Experian and TransUnion). A credit freeze blocks most people and companies from looking at your credit report without your permission.

When a credit freeze won't help

A credit freeze is designed to help prevent *future* identity theft by putting an obstacle in front of criminals trying to establish new loans or credit. A credit freeze won't prevent someone from making purchases on your *existing* credit-card accounts or making debit-card or other withdrawals from your *existing* checking account.

Who is the best candidate for a credit freeze?

If you won't need access to credit or a credit-dependent service in the near future and are worried about identity theft, you are probably a good candidate for a credit freeze. It is best suited for seniors who aren't applying for new credit but it can be very useful for many, many people (especially in our age of identity theft).

Living with a credit freeze

A credit freeze, however, can complicate your life somewhat because most companies want to see your credit report before hiring you, renting you an apartment, giving you insurance, setting up telephone and utility services, issuing a credit card or making a loan to you.

With a credit freeze, access by others to your credit reports is cut off unless you unfreeze the freeze. Note that companies you already have an existing relationship with (for example, a credit-card company, a bank or a utility service) may still want to view your reports for creditworthiness.

There *may* be a fee for unfreezing unless you have a police report showing you were a victim of identity theft or some exception applies in your state (e.g., being a senior or under the age of 19 in some states).

Depending on what state you live in, your credit freeze may automatically expire after a certain number of years (e.g., seven years) making it necessary for you to calendar when to reapply for the freeze.

At this time, fewer than half of the states allow a parent or guardian to place a credit freeze on a minor's credit report.

Unfreezing your credit

If you know a company will be checking your credit, find out which of the three agencies they'll use so you only need to unfreeze that one credit report. You can do a temporary unfreeze for a specified period of time or a permanent unfreeze.

Although an unfreeze is supposed to be instantaneous, sometimes it can take weeks by mail if the online unfreeze (or unfreeze over the telephone) doesn't work for whatever reason.

*****

Credit-Monitoring / Identity-Theft Services

At some point you may decide to sign up for a credit-monitoring service to let you know whether there is a change in your credit status, an unauthorized address change or public filings against you such as a lien. The monitoring service may also tell you your credit score and provide other services and benefits.

These monitoring services vary in how they work and how extensive their protection is.

A more extensive service will watch for address changes and fraudulent activity in your name including credit cards, lines of credit and mortgages as well as monitor dark web and black market websites and your financial accounts for unusual activity.

Most of these services are *after-the-fact* services that tell you a problem has already occurred. They don't prevent someone from getting credit or opening an account in your name. Contrast that with a credit/security freeze which is designed to help prevent new problems.

This type of service may or may not monitor other types of identity theft. For example, someone may take out utility services in your name and you won't know a problem occurred until the delinquent account goes to collection.

In addition, a service may monitor the use of your name to see whether it appears in court and other public records and even databases such as the ones for sex offenders (i.e., where someone who is arrested gives your name).

How these services may differ

- Some cover only one credit-reporting service (Equifax, Experian or TransUnion) while others cover all three services.

- The reporting to you may be daily, weekly or monthly or in real time.

- The cost for the services can differ.

- Some services make you aware of new accounts opened in your name.

Before selecting a service

- Make sure identity-theft insurance is included and confirm the amount of the insurance and what it covers.

- See if you have limited or unlimited access to your credit reports and credit scores (which may not include your FICO score). (For more on the FICO score, see Credit Scores below.)

- If you were to suffer identity theft, ask in advance how much help they would offer contacting the appropriate agencies and companies and providing legal assistance.

- Find out about the extent of the monitoring and whether it includes public records, online directories of information, search engines, blogs, online chat rooms and any other sources.

- Ask about the cancellation policy for the service.

Free monitoring services after a security breach

If you are given free credit monitoring after a breach of a database, find out whether it covers just one or all three of the credit reporting agencies (Equifax, Experian and TransUnion). Also ask how long the protection will last: one year, two years or as long as you continue to do business with the company that had the breach.

There may be more than one level of protection. See whether (a) you can get the highest level of protection (and not just the basic level) at no cost to you and (b) you are automatically notified when there is any activity on your credit reports.

*****

Identity-Theft / Cyber Insurance

In this day and age, it is prudent to have identity-theft insurance. First see whether your homeowners, renters or business policies have sufficient identity-theft insurance coverage and help resolve any breaches. If not, you may want to get a separate policy or one through an identity-monitoring service. Newer cyber policies may also include home-security audits to see whether your computer and home network are vulnerable.

Before you get your policy, first check out the following:

- Whether losses that occurred before the policy's initial effective date but discovered after that date are covered
- The amount of the coverage (and deductible, if any) and whether it covers not only your actual financial losses from identity theft but also all related attorneys' fees, lost wages and costs to document your losses
- Which types of identity theft are covered or not covered
- How they clear and restore your good name
- Whether any claim on this type of policy can cause an increase in your premium for any other insurance you have with the same company

*****

Business Identity Theft

Business identity theft can happen if a criminal poses as an owner, officer or employee of a company to illegally get money, merchandise, loans or credit in the name of the business or steal proprietary information.

Don't think that only big companies are targets. More than 70% of cyberattacks happen to businesses with fewer than 100 employees.

What you as a business owner can do for protection

- Get professional advice on securing computer systems to protect your business and client information, trade secrets and intellectual property.

- Keep all your software up to date.

- Do regular security scans.

- Determine which computers with sensitive and/or financial data should *always* be kept offline.

- Encrypt your data.

- Use Two-Factor Authorization (2FA) instead of just passwords for more security.

- Check the security standards of vendors.

- Train employees on safe workplace cyber habits (which websites to avoid, which links to avoid clicking, which scam emails and phone calls to avoid responding to)

- Get comprehensive business insurance that covers any potential theft losses; include cyber insurance with coverage for losses you suffer through takeovers of financial accounts, business interruption costs and exposure of customer/client confidential information.

- Periodically check your business filings to see how they read in the records of the Secretary of State, County Recorder, Dun & Bradstreet, Equifax, Experian and TransUnion.

- Shred unneeded business records rather than putting them in the trash.

- Report business identity theft to police and small business reporting agencies (Dun & Bradstreet, Equifax, Experian and TransUnion.).

*****

Ransomware

Whether you're an individual or someone with a business, you may encounter a "ransomware" demand. Such a demand happens when malware infects your computer and prevents your access to your data unless you pay a ransom to release the hold on your information. Ransomware usually comes through an email. There are even reports of doctor's offices encountering patient databases encrypted by cybercriminals demanding ransom payments.

If you have a good backup of your data, you can be better prepared to withstand a ransomware demand by wiping your device clean (if possible) and restoring your data or just getting another device and putting the backed-up information on it.

Since your backups may become infected, for local non-cloud backups, it's most protective to have an external backup drive plugged in only while you're doing a backup (e.g., once a day). Use a backup program that also saves older versions of files (*versioning*) in case only newer versions are infected.

Some ransomware out there has bugs so files aren't recoverable even by the hacker. This is all the more reason to have a good backup of your information.

*****

Credit Reports

Keeping good credit—what's in it for you?

Just as you use a passport to identify yourself to enter another country, your credit report and your credit score identify you to lenders, employers, landlords and others who want to know more about you. It's not the only tool they use to judge you, but it is a common one.

It's a good idea to get your reports in order several months before you plan any action or transaction that will involve providing a credit report to make sure everything is accurate.

Credit report vs. credit score

A credit report is a dollars-and-cents report of your credit history that shows how well (or poorly) you've been doing in paying your bills, how much debt you've taken on and how long you've had the debt.

Credit reports are often used by lenders, landlords, employers and insurance companies in making decisions about you. When it comes to your car insurance, your credit score may be more important than your driving record in setting your insurance-premium cost.

This type of report contains a lot of specific dollar details as well as public information records such as bankruptcies and tax liens.

The three main credit reporting agencies are:

Equifax, www.equifax.com
Experian, www.experian.com
TransUnion, www.transunion.com

Getting free copies of your credit report

Each year you can (and should) get a free copy of your credit report from each of the three credit-reporting agencies at https://www.annualcreditreport.com/index.action (or 1.877.322.8228).

You can either get them all at once or spread them out during the year.

The advantage of spreading them out, say one report every four months, is that you will receive periodic updates of what's happening with your report and can spot any needed corrections several times a year.

In some cases, you may be able to get additional free reports if (a) your report has inaccurate information because of identity fraud, (b) you've been denied credit, or (c) you're unemployed and want to apply for employment in the next 60 days.

Who has access to your credit report

Employers, landlords, insurance companies, companies that have extended you credit or may be doing so and others can get a copy of your report. Generally, employers need your permission to get the report.

Errors in your credit report

You'll want to quickly correct errors in your report by contacting the credit-reporting agency in writing via certified mail, return receipt (keeping a copy of your correspondence, of course). In some cases, the credit-reporting agency may be confusing you with someone else. In other cases, someone is impersonating you and causing items to appear in your report.

You may want the corrected report sent to anyone who has received an incorrect report in the prior six months (and up to two years for employers).

Correct but negative information

Even if a report is correct, certain negative information (e.g., bankruptcies) should be automatically removed over time.

Note that for any item that does remain in your file, you can include a short statement to explain the item.

For more information on deleting information, see http://www.experian.com/blogs/ask-experian/when-negative-information-will-be-removed-from-your-credit-report/

*****

Credit Scores

A "credit score" is a three-digit number (higher is better) that lenders and others use to help them determine whether you're a good credit risk. Also known as a "risk score," the most widely used one is the FICO from Fair Isaac (www.myfico.com). The three credit-reporting agencies also offer a credit score. There is generally a fee for receiving your credit score.

Very often, employers, insurance companies, landlords and others will want to see your credit report *and* your credit score to assess your reliability.

*****

Credit-Fixing Services

Be wary when using a credit-repair service. First see Credit Repair: How to Help Yourself at www.consumer.ftc.gov/articles/0058-credit-repair-how-help-yourself

*****

What to Do When Identity Theft Occurs

Time is of the essence. Act quickly to get needed legal advice and to minimize the damage you suffer.

Identity theft can take time to clear up. In the meantime, it may be difficult for you to get credit, rent an apartment or possibly get a new job.

If you're a victim of identity theft, keep good records of all phone calls and correspondence in your handling of the investigation and the restoration process. With each contact, write down the name and title of who you spoke to, their employee number, the date and time of the conversations, the name of the company, what phone numbers you called, what was said and the confirmation number for the conversation.

Whenever you mail information, send it certified mail, return receipt requested. Dispute incorrect and fraudulent charges in writing and in a timely manner.

Also see http://www.consumer.ftc.gov/features/feature-0014-identity-theft

The main steps to take

Figure out what has been breached. Does the breach involve credit, debit or ATM cards, your existing financial accounts, new accounts established in your name, your Social Security number or your driver's license number?

Get legal advice as needed on all of the following steps before taking them:

- If you have identity-theft insurance, contact the company for advice on the steps to take and whether you or the insurance company will need to take those steps.

- File an identity-theft police report and request a form for getting information from creditors and other businesses regarding the fraud.

  With a police report, you should be able to:

  Have fraudulent/inaccurate information blocked from your credit reports as well as collection-agency actions and inquiries.

  Receive a copy of all application and transaction records on all accounts opened fraudulently in your name.

  Get a free credit freeze and/or a seven-year fraud alert from the three credit-reporting companies.

- Report fraud quickly to the fraud department of the affected companies to hopefully limit or eliminate your liability by cancelling the affected accounts.

- Get a copy of your credit report from each of the three credit-reporting agencies (Equifax, Experian and TransUnion) and look for new, unauthorized accounts to report. Also check your address, phone number and employment information listed on the report.

- Ask the companies not to report the fraudulent accounts to the three credit-reporting agencies.

  Ask them to notify anyone who received your credit report during the past six months (two years for employers) to alert them to the fraud and incorrect information. Make sure they do remove the incorrect information and eliminate the fraudulent accounts, addresses, birth date, phone number and other information submitted by the imposter.

Get a letter confirming that not only have the fraudulent accounts been closed but there are no amounts owed on the closed accounts.

Have the affected companies send you their fraud packet if they have one as well as any fraud-related documents they have. Advise them they are not to sell, exchange or donate your information for collection purposes while the investigation is ongoing.

- The Federal Trade Commission (FTC) is the governmental agency that oversees identity theft issues. You can report identity theft to the FTC at: https://www.ftccomplaintassistant.gov/#crnt&panel1-1

  An FTC Identity Theft Victims' Complaint and Affidavit is at: http://www.consumer.ftc.gov/articles/pdf-0094-identity-theft-affidavit.pdf

- Eliminate automatic payments on the closed accounts and set up automatic payments on the new accounts.

- Start daily monitoring by text or email alerts for activity on your cards and accounts.

- Calendar and make sure you get the monthly statements on your financial and credit-card accounts.

- If you get any phone call about the breach, be careful as it may be from the impersonator. To play it safe, don't give out information and instead call back to a company's fraud department. In general, you want to deal with the fraud department and not with general customer service.

- On checking accounts, have the bank or other financial institution (a) stop all outstanding (unpaid) checks that you didn't sign or authorize and (b) report the fraudulent activity to ChexSystems (which is a check-reporting agency). You may also want to report an identity-theft security alert directly with ChexSystems at https://www.chexsystems.com

- If your driver's license is affected by the fraud, contact the Department of Motor Vehicles (or other issuing agency) to alert them to the fraud to see if a new license with a different number can be issued to you and an alert can be placed on your account.

- If medical identity theft is involved, get a new health insurance policy number.

- For student loans taken out in your name, you can contact the Department of Education at 1.800.647.8733.

- Don't pay a bill or invoice that is not yours.

- If debt collectors contact you on unpaid, fraudulent bills, let them know that you are a victim of identity theft and that you are not responsible for the bills. Get the name of the person contacting you, their company's name, address and phone number and the information on the creditor. Write debt collectors (via certified mail, return receipt requested) about the identity theft and have them confirm in writing that you do not owe any money on the disputed bill.

- If you discover that someone has been arrested or convicted of a crime in your name, received traffic or parking tickets in your name or had a civil judgment entered under your name, get legal advice on how to resolve the situation including clearing your name in court records, criminal databases, your state's identity theft registry and the records of information brokers. Ask whether there is an Identity Theft Passport program in your state so you can present a card "of innocence" to law enforcement if they suspect you committed the crimes done by the imposter.

*****

Removing Your Information from the Internet

Sorry. There's no foolproof way to remove your information that's already out on the Internet. Much of the information on you is public information available from government sources.

However, in Europe, the "right to be forgotten" means that if you want search engines to remove search results referring to your name, you can file a request with the search-engine operator. Your request will be evaluated and you can appeal a result with a court.

Public records in the U.S.

There are federal, state, county, city and other public-entity public records.

Most states offer programs to keep information confidential and ways to seal court records where individuals need it for their personal safety.

Having said that, depending on the laws of a city, county and state, people may be able to find out your full name, address, birth date, dates of marriage, divorce records, arrest records, death certificate, Social Security number, driver's license number, addresses of all property you own, certain court records and more. School records are usually confidential.

The main federal privacy law is the Privacy Act of 1974. States have privacy laws, too. There are also "freedom of information" laws that can allow access to federal records including your seeing your own records.

There is no single source that lists where your records are in the federal system.

Some governmental records are sold to employers, insurance companies and others.

*****

DNA

Do you know where your DNA is? For example, since 1983 the State of California has been collecting and keeping the DNA of every person born in the state as part of a heel test at birth to detect congenital disorders.

Your DNA may not stay with the California Department of Health because it can sell DNA to private companies without your consent. That can be a real concern because some researchers say anonymized DNA can be cross-referenced using online data to connect it to a name.

Note that you can request that your child's DNA be destroyed—see the form at:

https://www.cdph.ca.gov/pubsforms/forms/CtrldForms/cdph4410.pdf

*****

Getting and Keeping a Job

When it comes to employment, the Internet can be a lifesaver or a nightmare. Follow these tips for a better experience.

Employment scams

Internet employment scams often start out with a phony job posting. Especially with online job searches, be protective of your Social Security number, credit-card number and bank-account information.

If you get involved with an employment scam as a potential or actual employee, it often ends up with your new employer asking you to transfer money. If you just remember that you are trying to find a job and not become a bank, you may steer clear of trouble.

These money scams usually have you using your existing checking account or a new one to deposit a check from the employer's "customers" and sending a portion of the deposit back to the employer. Unfortunately, those checks, cashier's checks or money orders you deposit are not real but the money that you send from your account is.

Many other employment scams involve your Social Security number so be on alert if you're asked for your number over the phone, on a cover letter or from a company located outside of the United States. It's best to first research a company (on www.bbb.org and www.lookstoogoodtobetrue.com and call the employer's HR department); then wait for a person-to-person interview where you can assess the situation before revealing your Social Security number.

Contact an employer's human-resources department to find out the company's proper hiring procedure and how you should submit your information. Human interaction is always the best policy. The more you can do face to face, the better chance you'll have to see if it's a real company that's worthwhile.

Online resumes

Along with false job postings, you should also be careful about what information you put on any resume, especially an online resume.

The golden rule is to post online only what you want an identity thief to see. The more generic the resume, the better protected you will be. Think twice before posting a video resume.

With online resumes, avoid posting your:

1. Social Security number (or Employer Identification Number if you use that for your work)
2. Driver's license number
3. Birth date
4. Birth place
5. Marital status
6. Gender
7. Street address
8. Phone number
9. The email address you use for financial or sensitive personal matters
10. Current employer
11. Detailed work history
12. Professional license numbers
13. References
14. College name (it's easy for someone to contact a college and get your information from a college directory) and graduation date—having said that, many people are comfortable providing their college name

For an online resume, have mail sent to a post-office box rather than your home address and use a separate, disposable email address that can be deleted when the job search is over.

Five important questions to ask before you post a resume

Ask the site (or find out the answers in the FAQs) to the following questions:

1. Will the resume stay online for a limited period of time?

2. Can you delete or revise a resume?

3. Are resumes shared with other job sites? (This can affect whether you can delete your resume.)

4. Can you mask your contact information so your personal information is kept anonymous?

5. What is the privacy policy for resumes and personal information?

Background checks

Employers may want to do a background check on you before you're hired.

Some employers check very extensively, requesting credit reports, character references, past employer references, names of neighbors, education records, workers compensation records and more.

A Work Number Employment Data Report lists the name of each employer, when you worked for the employer, your salary and your job title to verify your employment and income history. Most employers don't participate in providing this data on you.

You can get a copy of your own Employment Data Report to check at https://www.theworknumber.com/Employees/DataReport/index.asp

Get a copy of your credit reports

Get a copy of your credit reports from Equifax, Experian and TransUnion well before applying for a job. You want to have enough time to correct any errors so the reports don't cause you to lose a chance for a job.

Why bother to get the credit reports even if you've lived the life of a saint? Someone else's information with the same or a similar name could be part of your report. You can also have a problem if someone has put down your Social Security number by mistake. And, there's always a chance that an identity thief has been doing mischief in your name.

Also, for any bad news that can't be corrected, you'll be in a better position to explain it if you know it's on a report. Note that if you are turned down for a position because of your credit report, an employer has to give you notice of how the report influenced the decision and give you a chance to respond.

Beyond credit reports, it may be a good idea to also check your online identity by doing online searches on yourself, including reviewing your social-networking sites.

Information on new hires

If you do get hired, be aware that information about you will probably be transmitted to the government.

The new-hire file contains information on all newly hired (and rehired) employees as reported by employers to each State Directory of New Hires (SDNH). Such information includes the following seven data elements:

- Employee name
- Employee Social Security number
- Employee address
- Start-of-work date

- Employer name
- Federal Employer Identification Number (FEIN)
- Employer address

Many states require additional information.

Spying by employers

Since laws vary by state, employers and employees should get legal advice as needed.

Generally, there isn't much workplace privacy for employees. Employees should assume any device provided by an employer is subject to monitoring. Read through the company workplace privacy policy.

Depending on the state laws where the workplace is located and the contents of its policy manual, office-computer searches, emails, telephone calls, voice-mail messages and website visits could all be fair game for monitoring. Video monitoring of you at work may be permissible, too (of course not in a bathroom or locker room).

Phone-call monitoring on traditional phones can include not only listening to a conversation but also knowing what numbers were called by using a device known as a "pen register."

It gets trickier if you use your own device at work. Sometimes an employer installs work-related software on the device. The office policy manual should spell out what can and can't be done. It's not always clear where to draw the line on these devices.

In some states, you have to give notice of a work-related phone call being monitored (or recorded) by having a beep tone or playing a recorded message. Personal calls shouldn't be monitored but there is that risk if employees make personal calls from work phones. A better course of action is to make your personal calls on your personal phone.

Remember, even when you delete emails or other messages, they may be available because they were backed up on the workplace system or server.

Social media

Depending on the state where your employer is located and the workplace policies, your employer may limit what you can post on social-media websites. Contact your HR (human resources) department to learn about your workplace's policy.

In some states, your employer may require you to reveal your user name and password on social-media accounts.

Health information

Although employers generally can't access your personal health information, self-insured employers may have more leeway.

Physical (snail) mail

If physical mail is sent to you at work, chances are your employer can open it even if it is marked "confidential" or "personal."

If you receive resumes

HR departments expect to get resumes over the Internet. Hackers have figured this out so viruses hidden in resumes are becoming more common. That's why it's a good idea to keep the HR department computers separate from the rest of the company network.

*****

Renting

Rental applications

Rental applications can be a great way for someone to obtain confidential information about you. It will usually include your Social Security number, driver's license number, employment information, bank account information, income information and past residential addresses.

With so many foreclosures and vacant properties around, one risk is whether you're really dealing with the owner or someone posing as the owner. Make sure you're not turning over your money and information to an imposter.

Credit reports

Since landlords will generally want to look at your credit report (from Equifax, Experian or TransUnion), order a copy first to make sure it's accurate and if necessary, make any necessary corrections.

Residential/tenant screening report

Besides credit reports, landlords often utilize a specialty report (e.g., a residential/tenant screening report) to evaluate tenant risk factors.

Such a report may include not only your credit history (i.e., open accounts and payment history) but also information on your tenant history, rental-payment history, bad-check history, bankruptcies, insurance claims made on homeowner's policies, rental and automobile policies, court cases against you (including those involving rentals), criminal history, driving history and other matters of public record. Since there are many screening companies, ask your potential landlord which one will be used.

You should be able to get a copy of your tenant screening report by directly contacting the reporting agency. As with other reports, be sure to correct inaccurate information.

Tenant score

A landlord may order a tenant score on you (similar to a credit-report score) or access an unlawful detainer registry to see whether you've ever been evicted.

Insurance history report

Landlords may also look at your insurance report.

The C.L.U.E. Personal Property report provides a seven-year history of losses associated with an individual and his/her personal property.

You can order a free report at https://personalreports.lexisnexis.com/fact_act_claims_bundle/landing.jsp

For a free insurance-history report every 12 months, go to http://www.verisk.com/underwriting/a-plus-underwriting-verisk-insurance-solutions.html

*****

Mail

Mail theft and your mail box

You might be making it easy for identity thieves to cause you problems if you have an outdoor mailbox (with or without a lock on it).

That outdoor box gets your banking, other financial and credit-card statements as well as maybe your driver's license renewal and passport.

At the very least have a locked mailbox at home. Better yet, for more security, get a Post Office box or a commercial mailbox. An added benefit is that when you go on vacation, your mail won't pile up at your residence (you can request a vacation hold by the Post Office).

You may even advertise your mail by putting outgoing mail in the box and raising the attached red flag to let the postal carrier (and criminals) know that there's mail in there to pick up.

Don't leave envelopes that contain checks in open mailboxes. The payee and the amounts can be altered on checks if you don't use a security, non-erasable pen.

A criminal can also steal your incoming or outgoing mail by contacting a bank, credit-card or other financial company and then posing as you to change the mailing address or filing a false change-of-address form.

Post Office mail-deposit boxes on the street

Some mail boxes are safer than others but in general, be very cautious using a mail box on the street that has a wide opening that could allow someone to fish for your mail with a coat hanger or other device.

If your mail is stolen

If your mail is stolen, you should do the following:

- Contact the Post Office's Postal Inspector (not the local Post Office manager).

- File a crime report with the police.

- Contact all your financial and credit-card companies and carefully monitor your statements.

- Review your credit reports at the three credit-reporting agencies.

- Consider placing a credit freeze.

- See if you can determine which bills you should have received but haven't.

Junk mail and offers for credit cards

You can register with the Direct Marketing Association's (DMA) Mail Preference Service (MPS) at https://dmachoice.thedma.org/# to opt out of receiving unsolicited commercial mail from many national companies for five years.

If you decide that you don't want to receive prescreened offers of credit and insurance, you can either opt out of receiving them for five years or permanently by calling 1.888.5OPTOUT (1.888.567.8688) or going to https://www.optoutprescreen.com/?rf=t

At www.dmachoice.org, the DMA also has an Email Preference Service (eMPS) to help you reduce unsolicited commercial emails for six years.

*****

Data Brokers and Data Compilers

Data brokers and data compilers specialize in compiling, collecting and selling information on you.

These companies may use information about you to help market products to you, verify your identity, detect fraud or provide information about you to law enforcement, organizations, the media or other consumers.

What information they have on you

The information they have on you may include your name, address (and whether you're moving), Social Security number, date of birth, gender, marital status (including whether you're getting married), phone number, religion, political affiliation, hobbies, medical conditions, occupation, educational level, estimated income level, whether you use credit and/or debit cards and your social media history. Whew! Did I leave anything out?

Although a lot of your information is already public through government records, you, your family and your friends may be volunteering a ton of information about you through social media and at websites where you log in to get information and services.

Opting out of the major data compilers

There are hundreds if not thousands of data brokers and compilers. Some will let you delete your information but others won't. The bottom line is that you can't remove your information from everywhere. Here are a few to start with:

- Acxiom, 1.877.774.2094 or www.acxiom.com/about-acxiom/privacy/us-consumer-choices/

- Epsilon Data Services www.epsilon.com/consumer-preference-center/

- To remove your name for five years or permanently from lists supplied by the consumer credit-reporting companies (Equifax, Experian, Innovis and TransUnion) for preapproved and prescreened offers of credit or insurance, call 1.888.567.8688 or go to https://www.optoutprescreen.com/?rf=t

*****

Specialty Reports

You may want to review at least some of your specialty reports to see what's in them to make sure they're accurate and there's no fraud being done in your name.

LexisNexis reports are used by businesses and the government. You can get a free copy of your report (ask for a Full File Disclosure) once a year at 1.866.868.9534 or https://personalreports.lexisnexis.com/access_your_full_file_disclosure.jsp

It includes CLUE insurance reports on you.

Other sources of specialty reports include the following:

- NCTUE (National Consumer Telecom & Utilities Exchange), which tracks your account histories and your phone and utilities usage; you can get a free copy of the NCTUE Disclosure Report at 1.866.349.5185 or www.nctue.com/consumers

- MIB Group "MIB" report, on your applications for individually underwritten life, health and disability policies at www.mib.com/request_your_record.html

*****

Dropping Off the Internet

You may fantasize or actually try to get yourself off the Internet. How would you do this?

- The first step would be removing your social-network presence from the Internet including Facebook, Twitter, LinkedIn and Google. If you can't end an account, you might change your information to something random.

- Your next step would be to try to remove your information from search engines (e.g., Google, Bing and Yahoo). Google has a removal tool.

- If you've posted on websites or blogs, see if you can get your posts removed.

- Next, delete your online shopping and cloud storage accounts.

- If you've posted on websites or blogs, see if you can get your posts removed.

- Have your landline and cellphone companies remove your information.

- Contact the information-collecting websites such Spokeo and PeopleFinder. You might hire a service that specializes in removing your public information.

- Delete your email accounts.

*****

Do Not Call Registry

Tired of those unwanted telemarketing phone calls? Sign up for the Do Not Call Registry at 1.888.382.1222 or https://www.donotcall.gov. Note that the registry does not stop political, charitable or survey calls.

Although unsolicited telemarketing calls are prohibited to cellphones, you might want to register your cellphone number, too.

*****

Malware

"Malware" is a shortened form of the words "malicious software" and it includes software such as a virus or Trojan horse that is designed to disrupt, damage or in some way harm computer systems. (Malware is sometimes referred to as "greyware.")

Computer infections come from malware programs that may, for example, let hackers see every keystroke (and password) you type and more.

Hackers may get access to all of the data and information on your computer (and maybe your network) and even turn your computer into a zombie as part of a "botnet" (secret network) that carries out attacks (or sends spam) to other computers without your knowledge.

There are many kinds of malware. A "virus" is a computer program that spreads through human interaction such as running the infected program. The most common way of getting a virus is by downloading an infected file.

A "worm" is like a virus but it is self-replicating and it can spread without human interaction once it's on a computer.

A "Trojan horse" looks like a useful program but it isn't. Ordinarily, it is not self-replicating and it does its mischief just on the computer where it's located. Trojan horses can spread in ways that resemble virus infections. A "RAT" (remote access Trojan) is a program that can take over a computer remotely.

Although there is no universally accepted definition of "spyware," it is generally considered to be (a) any program that monitors your computer activities (such as logging your keystrokes, keeping track of the websites you visit or capturing your personal data) or (b) a program that installs itself without your knowledge or permission. Examples include a "rootkit," which can install hidden files and user accounts and intercept data and a "keylogger."

A big growth industry is spying on your Internet usage. Besides cookies, more sophisticated techniques such as Flash cookies and beacons are tracking more of how you use the Internet. A "beacon" can monitor and store what you type on websites (e.g., comments on songs or personal interests) and even where your mouse goes. That data can then be sold (generally without disclosing your name).

How to avoid getting malware

The key steps are doing the following:

- Use a limited, standard user account rather than an administrator account (see Administrator Mode in Chapter 5).
- Avoid clicking on links in emails.
- Be very careful in deciding which files you download from emails or messages and scan them for malware before using them.
- Get your software from original vendors.
- Keep your operating system, antivirus, antispyware and other software up to date.
- Use two-factor authentication.
- Avoid less secure programs such as Flash.
- Use a more secure browser such as Google Chrome.

How to get rid of malware

The safest way to remove malware is to (a) have a good backup of your data; (b) format (actually reformat) the device (set it to the factory status that first came with the device when it was new); (c) reinstall the operating system and other software from a reliable source; and (d) get all needed software updates.

*****

Customer-Loyalty Programs

If you sign up for a supermarket or another customer-loyalty program, it may make sense to use a name other than your own to maintain your privacy. Better yet, skip these programs and maintain your privacy unless the benefits are just too good to pass up.

*****

Doxing

Doxing is the process of searching for and publishing on the Internet personally identifiable or private information. Research can include Internet and social-networking websites.

Doxing can be used for valid purposes (e.g., law enforcement) or improper purposes (e.g., public shaming).

It can put you in a difficult position. If you respond to the information, you may be authenticating it. It may be more useful to report it to online moderators, the email and ISP provider for the doxer or the police.

How to prevent doxing

The best steps to prevent doxing that applies to your Internet usage are:

- Use different names for each online profile—this makes it more difficult for people to put together information on you.

- Don't use your name or a portion of it in your email address, Facebook, Twitter or other online profile names (unless absolutely necessary for your benefit).

- Don't have your address, date of birth or place of birth online on any website. (Don't encourage birthday greetings to you.)

- When you post photos online, make sure the geotagging (location data) of the photos is disabled (you'll want to switch the location setting back to "on" when you use navigation, mapping or certain other apps).

- Don't accept friend requests or business-link requests from everyone—check them out first on the Internet.

- Be careful when clicking on any links or downloading files.

*****

Eavesdropping on You

There are several ways people can eavesdrop on you:

- By "bluebugging," hackers can eavesdrop on your telephone conversations as well as make calls, send and receive text messages and access the Internet on your phone.

- Voice search functions in smartphones send voice recordings over the Internet that could include private conversations.

- Older, analog cordless phones may make it easier for people to eavesdrop on your conversations.

- Some smart TVs using voice commands can store with a third party all of your conversations occurring in front of the TV.

- In addition, if your devices are responding to your voice commands through Apple's Siri, Google Now, Microsoft's Cortana or Amazon Echo or Alexa, they are always listening to you unless you turn them off. You may also be able to delete the service's recordings of you.

2. Credit, Debit and ATM cards and Financial Accounts

Credit Cards

Besides their convenience, credit cards offer other benefits. Paying by credit card may put you in a better position to deal with defective merchandise. Also your credit-card company may offer extended warranties on purchases made with the credit card.

The most important protection credit cards offer is the limitation of your liability for unauthorized use of your credit card to $50, if you protest unauthorized charges in writing in a timely manner (some companies won't charge you at all). Make sure your letter is received timely—well before 60 days of the mailing date of the statement (not within 60 days of the date you received the statement) containing the problem. Keep a copy of what you send and retain original documents (only send copies).

Double-check where to send your protest letter (via certified mail, return receipt requested) and the exact information to include. The address is probably not the same as the address for payments.

Other ways to protect yourself

- When shopping online, use a credit card and not a debit card or check.
- Use a separate credit card for online purchases to prevent possible contamination of your other credit cards and to make it easier to spot improper charges.
- One-time PINs or security codes sent to your cellphone may be used as a second layer of authentication.

- It's *not* a good idea to use a credit card online if you're using a hotspot connection. If you must do so, use a VPN (see Chapter 9). If you're in a public setting, look around to ensure no one can see what you're typing.

- If your Internet browser's autocomplete settings store your credit-card information or other personally identifiable information, you may be asking for trouble. Likewise, if a website wants to "remember" and store such information for the future, don't do it. While it takes a little inputting time, it's safer to provide this information for *each* transaction.

- Consider using a prepaid card for online purchases. Note, however, prepaid cards won't have certain benefits your other credit cards may have (e.g., extending the warranty on purchases). One other alternative may be one-time disposable credit card numbers available from your credit-card company.

- Calendar credit-card expiration dates so you can contact the company if a new card doesn't arrive on time.

- When you get your monthly credit-card statement, review it right away. First, match your receipts against the charges listed on the statement. Then double-check interest charges and any fees on it.

- Before you sign up for a card, read the terms and conditions of its use. A few cards now allow repossession of goods you buy if you don't pay your bills.

- Pay by cash whenever possible to reduce the number of businesses that have your credit-card information.

Four ways you may be surprised by your credit-card statements

1. Someone may be using your credit card without your permission.

2. A merchant may have charged you more than you agreed to pay or charged you twice for the same purchase.

3. Charges from someone else's card may have ended up on your statement.

4. The credit-card company may have charged you an incorrect interest rate or added charges that shouldn't be on the statement.

Dispute incorrect charges as soon as possible. The Federal Trade Commission advises sending a letter disputing charges so it reaches the creditor within 60 days after the first bill with the error was mailed to you. See http://www.consumer.ftc.gov/articles/0219-disputing-credit-card-charges

Credit cards with chips

Most credit cards now have chips embedded in them to reduce counterfeiting and onsite fraud at stores and other in person places you do business. Chips make it more difficult for fake credit cards to be created and used for in-store purchases.

The chip cards don't prevent online purchase fraud but they do protect you better for in-person transactions especially if the merchant uses "point-to-point encryption" (where your card's data is unlocked only after it reaches the payment processor).

Whether the chips are more protective depends on the credit card hardware your merchant is using. Not all terminals can take the newer chip cards. Some prepaid cards have the chip, too.

The good news is that cards with chips generate a one-time dynamic code when they are used (Older cards with only a magnetic strip in them have static information that doesn't change).

Some banks are also requiring a PIN with the newer chip cards for additional protection.

These newer cards may present an opportunity for scammers to get your information. Criminals may email or call you saying they need your credit card and personal information to issue a new chip card. Don't respond directly to these contacts. Instead, call the 800 number on the back of your credit card to determine what needs to be done.

Electronic pickpocketing

It is unlikely someone with a scanner will pick up information from your credit cards even if they are RFID-enabled. However, if you're really worried about electronic pickpocketing (also known as "RFID skimming"), wrap your cards in aluminum foil or an RFID-blocking wallet. Keep in mind that you're much more likely to encounter ATM skimming than RFID skimming.

Opting out of credit card offers

Unless you want to see them, opt out of mailed prescreened credit-card and insurance offers (either for five years or permanently) at 1.888.567.8688 or https://www.optoutprescreen.com/?rf=t which covers the lists at the three main credit-reporting agencies; otherwise, your mailbox may fill up with offers that criminals may get their hands on.

*****

Debit Cards

Debit cards are an interesting mixture. They look like a credit card but they function like a check.

A debit card is really electronic money. When you use a debit card to make a purchase, the money to pay for the purchase is taken out of your account right then electronically.

Be aware that some merchants (e.g., hotels and rental-car companies) do "merchant blocking" with debit cards where a certain amount is deducted from your checking account even before the transaction is completely processed. As a result, you may have less money available in your account than you thought.

Credit cards may be better to use than debit cards for three reasons. First, if there is fraudulent activity with your card, the law provides greater protection for you with a misused credit card. That's a very good reason not to use a debit card for online purchases. Second, paying by credit card may put you in a better position to deal with defective merchandise. Third, your credit-card company may offer extended warranties on purchases made with the credit card.

If you lose your debit card, someone could potentially empty out your bank account using your card. Ideally, minimize your use of debit cards.

Even if you report a lost or stolen debit or ATM card (or unauthorized use of one) within two business days to your bank, it can take two weeks (or possibly longer) to put the funds back in your account. In the meantime, you may have bounced checks, incurred fees and lost access to your funds to pay your rent, mortgage and other bills.

Liability with unauthorized use of a debit card

The most protective policy is report the loss or theft of a card immediately. If you report the theft or loss of a debit card to your bank before any fraudulent use happens, you are not responsible for the unauthorized charges. You should always report a loss or theft not only by phone as soon as possible but also in writing via certified mail, return receipt requested.

If you report it within two business days, your liability is limited to $50. (Some companies won't charge you at all but don't count on it.)

If you report it after the two-day deadline and have it received before 60 days from the time your bank statement was mailed, your liability limit is $500.

However, if you report it too late, you could lose all of the money in your checking account (and possibly more if you have overdraft protection).

*****

ATM Cards and ATMs

ATM cards are a great convenience and a potential security issue. On the spectrum of risk, credit cards are safer than ATM cards and ATM cards are safer than debit cards.

Be on the lookout for ATM PIN skimmers

Thieves want to know your PIN to make withdrawals from your accounts.

ATM cards aren't foolproof. Thieves may install a device known as a skimmer on ATM machines to capture your account number and PIN. That's why you want to be sure to cover the keypad with your other hand when entering a PIN.

Safety precautions for ATM cards

- Memorize your PIN so you don't carry the number on you.

- Use a unique PIN for each account.

  Don't use the PIN as your email password, for other sensitive accounts or on any of your social networking websites.

- Take your ATM receipts with you when you leave the machine.

  Compare them to your checking account transactions. Better yet, set up text alerts so you know right away if your card has been used.

- Keep your ATM transactions private.

  Ask people to please move back if they are too close to you and can see what you're doing.

- Don't use just any ATM.

  Rely more on ATMs at bank locations. Be especially careful at gas stations and outdoor ATM machines. At night, only use ATMs that have good lighting and safe conditions or just wait until the next day.

Some ATMs work differently. You don't bring your ATM card with you. Instead, you call up to schedule a withdrawal and the ATM machine identifies you by scanning your iris or a bar code that has been sent to your phone. With this approach, you can minimize your time (and security risk) standing at an ATM. A thief trying to use your stolen phone would usually need to unlock your password-protected phone, sign into your mobile wallet or bank app and generally know your PIN—that's not easy to do.

*****

PayPal

Services such as PayPal allow you to use your credit card but shield its identifying information from the payee.

*****

Cash

Paying by cash is so yesterday but it could save you a lot of aggravation tomorrow.

Paying by cash keeps your purchases more anonymous as compared to using a credit card, debit card or check.

Naturally, cash can't be used for every purchase (and shouldn't be such as where you may later want proof of payment with a cancelled check or where you can get a free extended warranty through a credit card purchase).

*****

Online Banking

Virtually every bank allows you to bank online. What this means is that via the Internet you can pay certain bills electronically, move your money among different accounts and check your balances.

To bank online, you either need to use the bank's software with your computer (or mobile device) or access your account through the Internet.

With online banking, credit cards or other financial or sensitive information, only use websites that start out with "https" because they are more secure than "http" sites.

The "s" after http stands for "secure." A secure site is designed to encrypt your information or other data while it's traveling between your Internet browser and the website's server.

An *https* site should have a *lock icon* in the Internet browser (not on the Web page itself) with the lock in the closed position.

One advantage of banking online is that you can set up and receive alerts when there is activity in your accounts so you may be totally aware of any activity (by you or by a criminal) in virtually real time. (The same is true for your credit-card accounts, too.)

With online banking, you need to be sure you keep your device's security, operating system and general software up to date and that you do regular virus and spyware scans. It's safest to have a separate computer that you only use for financial websites and email.

Avoid handling your banking using a public computer or your device at wireless hotspots that may not be secure.

Also, when you log out of a public computer, don't just close down the Internet browser (e.g., Internet Explorer); instead, completely log off and restart the computer to wipe out traces of your online activity. Even with that, you are taking a tremendous risk in using a public computer for financial matters.

*****

P2P Payments

These payments are usually part of an app and allow you to send and receive payments from another person or company.

To transact P2P payments, you may need to know the bank account and routing numbers or just the email address and cellphone number of the other person or entity.

As with mobile payments, the levels of your protection depend on the payment mechanism you use (e.g., credit card, debit card, etc.).

*****

Checking Accounts and Check Fraud

Five main types of checking-account fraud

1. With "check washing," a thief gets hold of a check you have filled out and signed and then uses chemicals to change the name of the payee and the amount or to order a set of your checks.

2. With a "checking account takeover," the thief becomes a signer on the account and changes the mailing address.

3. With a "check theft," a thief uses one or more of your unused checks.

4. With "check counterfeiting," a thief creates checks with your account's information.

5. With "check synthesizing," a thief uses your name and address on an account you didn't open.

Checking-account fraud

Checking-account fraud can be tricky to detect because there is no one system for retail stores to verify checks.

You may discover a problem when

- You don't receive your usual monthly statement.

- You do receive a statement but it shows checks, transfers and deposits unknown to you or bearing someone else's signature.

- You receive a notice or letter from a merchant, a financial institution or a district attorney about a problem check.

- You get a tax statement from a bank where you don't have an account

- You get a notice from a bank or financial institution for an account change you didn't authorize.

How to help prevent checking-account fraud

- Use checks in numerical order so it's easier to tell which ones have been stolen.

- Have a strong, unique, complex password and PIN number on your account.

- When you write a check, don't leave empty space on the payee line for someone to add their name as a payee (e.g., changing the payee from "Susan Jones" to "Susan Jones *or John Smith*"). Likewise, don't leave extra space at the beginning of the lines where you write the amount. For examples, *don't* do this:

  ______________________ Forty Dollars and $^{00}/100$

  Someone could change the amount to say

  Five hundred and Forty Dollars and $^{00}/100$

  Better to start writing your amount as far left as possible and adding a line to go to the end to prevent changes:

Forty dollars and------------------------ 00/100

- Use a pen with *nonerasable ink* so the payee and amounts can't be changed.

- Monitor your statements right away—you have a limited amount of time to report fraud.

- As part of opening an account, get checks that only have your first initial and your full last name rather than your full first and last names. For a similar reason, you may want to get checks without your address or at least without your phone number. When you open a checking account, never have your Social Security number preprinted on checks.

- For added security, pick up new checks directly at the bank or other financial institution, if possible, rather than having them mailed to you.

- Have your mail sent to a post office box or a locked mailbox at home.

- Shred older, unnecessary checks with a cross-cut (or micro-cut) shredder.

- Use a credit card instead of a check since there is more protection if credit-card fraud occurs.

What to do in response to check fraud

- Notify the fraud department of the bank right away both by phone and in writing (using certified mail, return receipt requested). To save you time and aggravation, just speak to fraud investigators. Place a stop payment on stolen/misused checks and have your bank flag stolen checks and request that the checks be turned over to law enforcement to clear your name and find the thief.

- Keep good notes of the phone calls you make to report the fraud (i.e., the phone number you called, the time of the call, who you spoke to including the person's title and employee number and the case or incident number the person gives you), the steps you've taken, what has been done to resolve the problem and who will do what next and what remains to be done. Get copies of problem checks and keep copies of all correspondence.

- Have the bank credit you for the affected funds.

- Have the fraud department close the account. Get a letter of clearance or other written confirmation from your bank that the account has been closed and is marked "closed due to theft and not to be reopened." Keep this information in your permanent records.

- Open a new account, safeguard its information and use a strong, unique, complex password. See if you can add an extra password or some other additional protection to prevent problems on the new account. (If you have automatic payments made from the closed account, be sure to have payments tied to the new account.)

- Have the bank notify the check-reporting companies about the check fraud and verify to you when it has been done.

- Notify these check-reporting companies and request a free credit report from them:

    - ChexSystems, https://www.chexsystems.com, 1.800.428.9623

    - TeleCheck, www.firstdata.com/telecheck/telecheck-consumer-contacts.html or 1.800.366.2425

    - Certegy, https://www.askcertegy.com/FACT.jsp or 1.866.543.6315

- Notify the three credit-reporting agencies—Equifax, Experian and TransUnion—and make sure your records are corrected.

- If a criminal warrant has been issued in your name for a bad check, get legal advice on contacting the financial institution or merchant to withdraw the warrant and send you a letter of non-responsibility for the charges.

*****

Bills

No one likes receiving bills. However, it can be worse if you don't receive one.

One technique criminals use is changing your mailing address so you don't see charges on your credit cards or withdrawals from accounts for as long as possible.

Consequently, you need a system for calendaring your personal (and business) bills so you can ensure bills have arrived.

For example, make a master list of due dates (e.g., in a Word file) showing when recurring bills should be received (e.g., credit-card bills, student-loan bills, insurance premiums, etc.).

Then if you don't receive a bill on time, whether due to a criminal changing your mailing address or the bill being lost in the mail, you can contact the creditor to find out the due date and the amount due and pay the bill on time to avoid any blemish on your credit record.

And don't put off looking at your bank, credit card and other financial statements (as well as your cellphone statement) and checking for fraudulent use of your accounts.

*****

Wallets and Purses

Do the following:

- Minimize the number of credit and debit cards that you carry.
- Don't carry your Social Security card with you.
- Don't carry your Medicare card with you (except on days you absolutely must carry it to get medical care) because it includes your Social Security number.
- Make a photocopy of the information in your wallet or purse (and place it in a secure place) so you'll know what is missing and who to call if your wallet or purse is lost or stolen.

*****

Secure Payment Agents

A way to pay online for purchases or bills is with a "secure payment agent" (SPA). An SPA replaces your real personal and financial information with anonymous information that isn't traceable back to you. If you use an SPA, make sure it has multi-authentication verifying your identity.

3. Passwords, Security Questions, 2FA and Biometrics

Passwords

You need to put some effort into choosing your passwords because attackers will use any personal information they have on you (e.g., personal information you or others post on social-networking sites, names and addresses in your contact list/address book, your zip code or important dates in your life) to invade your life.

These days, to restrict access to your computer and your files, you may be able to have fingerprint, retinal or facial-information scanning as a substitute for typing a password. But if you're like most of us, passwords are your primary way of restricting improper use of your identity, computer and mobile devices.

Give some thought and use some imagination in setting up your passwords because if your password is easy to remember, it's also generally easy to crack. Also, see below for tips on handling security questions if you forget your passwords.

Select and use passwords carefully

- Have *strong* passwords on *all* of your devices. There are programs that randomly generate tough passwords that you can use.

  Use more complex passwords (a combination of at least fifteen upper and lowercase letters, numbers and keyboard symbols) to provide greater security. As passwords increase in length, they become more secure because the number of possible combinations for cracking them goes up, too.

Have at least one symbol character in the second through sixth position. If you only have one symbol or capital letter, don't make it the first or last character in your password.

Make each password significantly different from prior passwords.

Passwords should not contain real words or slang (in any language), actual names (a person's or a pet's), your mother's maiden name, addresses, email addresses, phone numbers, birth dates or anything someone could learn from doing an Internet search on you or looking at your social-networking sites.

There are software programs known as "password crackers" that can easily decipher primitive passwords.

You can make your password much more secure if you use random, unmemorable passwords with letters, numbers and symbols.

- Change your passwords at least several times a year but don't weaken them in the process. Also, don't use a pattern that links the old passwords to the new ones.

- Use different passwords and variations for different websites and programs.

- Although it's a pain to come up with and keep track of different passwords and to change them on a regular basis, you're just asking for trouble if you don't carefully manage your passwords.

- Don't reuse passwords.

- Be careful with security/secret questions that allow your password to be retrieved or changed. If the answers to the questions can be found on the Internet, someone can impersonate you.

- If two-factor authentication (2FA) is available, use it. Some online services are no longer using passwords at all and instead just using a notification sent to your mobile device to allow you to log in.

- When accessing the Internet on a public computer (e.g., at a library), make sure you don't click "Remember my password." Otherwise, the next person using the computer may access your information. Delete the history of your Internet usage. When you log out, restart the computer to help wipe out traces of your computer use.

Store passwords securely

Although there are many password-manager programs (to track and store all of your passwords) that get good reviews from independent sources touting them as a secure way to store your online passwords, I still worry about having all of your passwords in one place on the Internet with a password manager. Some password managers change your passwords automatically on a regular basis.

Although there are password technologies including password synchronization, single sign-on (SSO) and portable, encrypted password tokens, I prefer keeping my passwords off my devices as handwritten or typed (but not saved on computer) hard copy in a secret place as well as in a safe deposit box.

Make sure your passwords aren't in your emails

If you get a confirming email for a new service or website that contains your password or you forget a password and request a reminder via email, there's a chance that your password(s) are still in an undeleted email.

If you have thousands of emails, it can be difficult to find those password emails. There are products to locate those emails.

Double security

You may prefer having more security with a fingerprint or other biometric device coupled with two-factor authentication and encryption.

Restrict automatic password completion

There are two kinds of "AutoComplete" where your device automatically types in information once you start to type. You probably want to keep the first kind—automatic completion of Web addresses you start to type in.

But you may not want to keep the second—having your passwords automatically typed in at websites. To prevent password AutoComplete, change the AutoComplete settings.

Doing so will also give you more protection if you lose your device or someone else gets hold of it. Besides disabling AutoComplete, you can also delete all the passwords that are already stored on your device.

Have password resets go to a special email address

To minimize problems, have a dedicated email address for receiving password resets if you forget your password(s). Have all password recovery actions go to that special email account; otherwise, if hackers get hold of your regular email account, they can reset your passwords by posing as you.

Be aware of automatic log-in dangers

Automatic log-ins allow anyone with access to your device to access its data. You may want to require a log-in when you start the device or if you put your device in sleep or hibernation mode.

Mac firmware passwords

It may not be enough to encrypt the files on your Mac with FileVault. You probably want to have a "firmware password." Setting a firmware password in OS X prevents your Mac from starting up from any device other than your designated startup disk.

Remember to put your firmware password in a safe place.

*****

Security Questions

Be careful how you answer security questions

Use the same care in selecting the questions (and answers!) you would in creating the password so it is not easily answered by anyone else.

Some websites (including nonfinancial websites) and apps require answers to security questions to verify your identity in the future if the need arises (for example, if you forget your password).

Be careful how you answer questions about your birthplace, birth date, driver's license number or mother's maiden name.

Correct answers may expose your vital identifying pieces of information to website hackers by allowing a hacker to pose as you.

Your privacy may be stronger if you intentionally use incorrect information in your answers. With so much of your information publicly available, it may make sense to make up (and write down!) unusual answers to security questions (e.g., Question: First car; Answer: 2xyT$w4!@$TR). Make sure you write down your incorrect "correct" answers since you may not be able to remember the intentionally wrong answers.

Of course, there are certain sites where you want to provide correct information.

*****

Two-Factor Authentication (2FA)

Passwords are one-step authentication and not very secure.

One of the best ways to protect your financial and sensitive accounts and information is using multi-factor authentication (also known as "two-factor authentication" or "2FA"). Two-factor authentication is an extra layer of security to ensure that you're the only person who can access your account, even if someone knows your password.

With 2FA, you need two ways to prove you are really you by having something you know (e.g., a password) and something you have (e.g., a phone). You'll provide a password *and* a code to access a service or website. The code is generally sent to your cellphone so assuming your phone isn't lost or stolen, you are better protected.

Three-factor authentication

For more security, three-factor authentication (3FA) is required in some cases. This involves a password, having a physical token or device (your phone) and biometric data about you such as a fingerprint scan or voiceprint.

*****

Application Specific Passwords

However, with 2FA turned on, some apps (e.g., mail apps on some phones) or devices (e.g., certain game consoles) will show a password error message because they can't prompt you to supply the security code when you log in. One way to handle this situation is to get and enter a unique app password (i.e., an application specific password).

There are risks with these app passwords. If you happen to use an app password with a malicious application or service, it could be used to access your entire account (e.g., Google, Microsoft, etc.) without requiring 2FA. This is more of a problem with older applications.

*****

Backup Codes

Backup codes, just like application specific passwords, allow you to bypass two-factor authentication (2FA). However, backup codes may only be used once whereas application specific passwords can be used repeatedly until you revoke them. Backup codes are set up as part of establishing 2FA and used to sign in if you lose your phone or otherwise can't receive codes via SMS, voice call, etc.

*****

Biometrics

In security matters, biometrics can identify you by using physical attributes such as retina, iris or voice scans, fingerprinting, facial characteristics, heart rhythms, patterns in finger or eye veins, posture, gait, body/bone signatures and even knuckles or noses.

Biometrics can be a substitute for passwords. But no technology is perfect when it comes to security. Some fingerprint readers accept images or fake fingerprints made out of gelatin. In addition, dirty or calloused fingers may not be read correctly. Consequently, iris scans are considered safer than fingerprints.

With some software, your movements, activities, social circles and possibly your emotions can be identified. In some cases, you can be identified even if your face is obscured or only the back of your head is seen.

Google and Facebook utilize facial recognition software. Google Photos can identify you in photographs. With Google, you opt in to allow facial recognition. Since Facebook identifies you as a default, you may want to adjust the settings to limit your being tagged in photographs.

Facial recognition has the downside that your face may be all over social media and available for others to use. That's why one bank is having customers scan their faces while speaking several numbers to see whether the lip movements match the sound. This is being done to be sure a face and not a photo is used for identification.

For any device that uses fingerprints, find out how the fingerprints are stored. Very often fingerprints are converted to a string of numbers and saved in a separate, "sandboxed" area, with restricted access, which is ideal.

Keep in mind that compromised passwords can be changed but your biometrics are permanent.

4. Email and Messaging Safety

Emails

Dangerous subject lines in emails

Email subject lines may not be all that friendly. Avoid opening emails that have no subject line or one that's too friendly or generic such as "Hi" or "Hello There." This is often a spam email that may inadvertently come from a friend's computer that has been infected with a virus. If you get an email with a suspicious or nonexistent subject line, call or email (without hitting "reply") first to confirm its validity before opening up the email.

Read email as plain text

Since malware can hide in HTML code, see if you can set your email program to show email as plain text (instead of as HTML) to reduce your online risks.

Make bcc part of your email ABCs

To prevent your email address from becoming part of a circulated list, encourage others to use the bcc (blind carbon copy) function in their email program. This allows the sender to email many people in one email but hide their email addresses. This prevents those addresses from being harvested by spammers and at the same time also helps prevent the spread of viruses. In turn, you can use the bcc function to restrict unnecessary broadcasting of email addresses.

Because spammers sometimes use the bcc function to send emails, some email programs automatically block bcc emails as junk emails. Recipients of your bcc emails may need to add your email address to their safe list for your bcc emails to get past their spam filters.

An alternative to using a bcc mass email is sending emails using the mail-merge feature, if your email program has this feature, so just one recipient's name appears in the "To" field of each email.

Don't "reply to all"

Your email program may allow you to disable the "Reply to All" option so recipients can't respond to everyone listed in the hidden bcc field by accidentally (or intentionally) clicking on "Reply to All."

Use two-factor authentication

To help prevent unauthorized access to your email, consider using two-factor authentication.

Recovering a hijacked email account

If someone takes over your email or social-networking account and changes the password, you may have a difficult time regaining control of your account. This can be more than an inconvenience since someone may send messages or do unlawful activity in your name.

Fortunately, the major email services and social-networking sites have recovery pages to help you regain control of your accounts.

Anonymous remailers

Using an anonymous remailer that receives your outgoing email, strips out your email address and then forwards it on to your recipient offers you some protection.

Fake email addresses

Your browser may have an add-on that lets you mask your email address by using a random, disposable address for a recipient website. Then any emails from that site will be forwarded to your actual email address.

Encrypting your email

Encrypting can be useful. Probably the best way to send secure email is with "end-to-end encryption" (two-way encryption) where only you hold the private key.

Different levels of protection for your email

If you send email and the government wants to look at the emails on your device, government officials need to get a warrant. However, access to your older email held by a third-party (i.e., your email provider), many agencies can issue their own subpoena on a lower standard than needed for a court-issued warrant. To top it off, you may not find out for weeks or months.

*****

Hotspots

Keep from getting burned at hotspots

You may use a wireless (e.g., Wi-Fi) connection at a hotspot (e.g., coffee shop, hotel or airplane) or even a wired network connection (e.g., at some hotels) to connect to the Internet. Some hotspots have better security protection than others. Be aware that even wired connections can be "sniffable" where sniffer software can penetrate the defenses of the network.

Therefore, as a first line of defense, try to minimize your use of hotspots, especially if you're dealing with sensitive information.

Another danger is the man-in-the-middle attack where a bad guy sends out a signal at the hotspot (e.g., coffee shop) so you use his wireless network and you'll reveal your passwords, credit-card and other vital information.

- Make sure your firewall is on to protect you.
- Avoid downloading software updates at hotspots since it may be malware and not a real update.
- Make sure your Wi-Fi settings don't allow your device to automatically connect with the nearest Wi-Fi access point.
- When not in use, turn off your wireless card.

Email at hotspots

If you're not using a VPN (Virtual Private Network), both your email login password and your emails may be vulnerable at hotspots unless you use some kind of secure connection.

When you check email at a hotspot, you're either using a Web-based account (e.g., Google's Gmail) or an email program that's on your device.

Web-based account

If you use a Web account to handle email, you can have a more secure login to protect your password by going to a login Web page that starts out as https:// rather than as http://. The "s" stands for "secure." Using a secure site to log in for your email keeps your password safer. However, you may then be redirected to a regular http site to read and send emails.

Find out whether you automatically stay on a secure site after logging in to protect the privacy of your email reading and sending. If not, see whether you can take steps to get more complete protection.

Email program

If you're using an email program that's on your device to check email at a hotspot with your ISP (Internet Service Provider), rather than the hotspot's ISP, see whether your ISP or email program offers a secure connection for checking email (secure POP3 or secure IMAP) or sending it (secure STMP).

However, if you must use the hotspot's ISP to connect to the Internet, it may not be that secure.

That's where a Web-based email service such as the secure connection for Gmail may be the safer way to go at a hotspot if you don't use a VPN.

Instant messaging

Try not to use instant messaging at hotspots since this is not the most secure method of communicating.

*****

Downloads

Be very cautious with downloads.

Avoid opening up files attached to emails or IMs from senders you do not know. Those files are a great way to infect your computer or mobile device. Use your common sense—if an email or IM looks or smells like trouble or you have an uneasy feeling, don't download or open it up.

Scan every download using antivirus software as soon as you have downloaded any file.

Warning on exe files

But even if you receive an attached file from a person you do know, don't download or open up a file that has an extension (i.e., ends with) exe in the name. Also, don't open or download files with two extensions.

Hidden file extensions

By default, Windows hides files extensions including "exe." You can view hidden file settings before opening a file to make sure it's safe. Whenever you see a double file extension or any extension that looks unusual (e.g., a pdf extension is not unusual), use care. Use your antivirus software to scan any file you download before opening the file.

*****

Links

Think twice before clicking on links in emails or IMs. Links are a common way to have malware infect your device.

For example, rather than clicking on a link to Facebook in an email, go to the Facebook website to log in. Otherwise, that link may take you to a malicious site instead.

*****

Search Engines and Your Email

The trend is to combine all of your information together whether it's your searches, email and other information.

For that reason, if you want more privacy, use separate companies as your email provider and your search engine so the two can't easily be connected up to one another. Also, use one browser for Internet searches and another one for your email.

*****

Alias Email Addresses

There are many times you are asked to provide your email address. In some cases, you may want to use an email alias to keep your privacy. See whether your email program allows you to create email aliases so you can give the alias email address when you don't want to give your real one to apps or websites. Another alternative is to create a junk email address just for this purpose.

*****

Instant Messaging

Instant messaging is not the most secure way of communicating, whether at work or at home. (Instant messaging is not the same as text messaging.)

Although instant messaging can be a great communication tool, it can also be an entry point to harm your computer or your network.

Remember that instant messages can be saved and stored on your devices just like emails and the automatic save feature is usually turned on.

Make sure you restrict your IM contacts to just your buddy list. Unless absolutely needed, keep IM simple and disable advanced features as well as file sharing and file transfer features.

Even if you don't save your IM conversations, the other party to the conversations may do so. In some cases, you can turn off your partner's saving feature by selecting an "off the record" option.

You may want to have a software program to help keep your instant messages confidential and to provide protection against unauthorized IM traffic.

You may get IM spam known as "spim." Try to avoid opening up those IMs and definitely do not click on links in the messages.

*****

Text Messaging

Your text messages may not be as secure as you'd like. To be secure, you want to have end-to-end encryption. That's where a message is encrypted before you send it and only the recipient can unencrypt it.

Some text messaging services have built-in default encryption that's automatically turned on. You also want the recipient to have the same level of encryption.

Even if your messages are secure, your metadata is probably vulnerable.

5. Safeguarding Your Computers and Tablets

You can do a lot to protect your computers and tablets. For brevity, I'm just using the term *computers* in this chapter. In some cases, the advice applies to cellphones, too.

Updates

One of the best steps you can take to avoid problems is to make sure the software on your devices gets all the available updates. For example, Verizon determined that 99.9% of hacks were due to a software bug that had been public for at least a year.

If you get a pop-up notice about updating, it's best not to click the update button. Instead, go to the website of the software or hardware vendor to download needed updates.

*****

Operating Systems

Choosing your operating system

The main software on your computer or other device is its operating system (e.g., Windows, Mac OS, Android, etc.). It allows software (e.g., your email program, Internet browser, word-processing program, etc.) to be installed and operated.

Over the years, Windows has been more of a target for hackers but no operating system is immune. It is essential that you install all updates for your device's operating system. Note that if you use the Windows XP operating system, Microsoft is no longer providing security updates.

Updating your computer's operating system

The operating system that came with your computer needs security updates from time to time to help keep you protected. Get the latest updates to your computer's operating system by going to the software company's site to download fixes and security updates or to use the automatic-update feature.

Generally, it's a good idea to use automatic updates for all of your programs. However, note that in 2016 Windows 10 will become a "Recommended Update" for devices with earlier versions of Windows. This means that if you have automatic updates and installations set up for your device, it will automatically upload Windows 10 and start its installer. See Chapter 11 for advice on this.

In some ways, your computer defenses come with an expiration date. If hackers discover flaws in your software (such as in firewall or antivirus software) and you don't have up-to-date versions, it may just be a matter of time until malware infects your computer. Instead, get software updates so your protection isn't compromised over time.

Download more than once if necessary

With operating-system updates, you may need to go back to the site more than once in one session and run additional checks because sometimes all the updates and fixes are not downloaded to your computer at one time. Keep checking until you are told on the screen that your computer is completely up to date.

Operating-system automatic updates may not be as automatic as you think

Generally, to keep your computer as secure and current as possible (and with the least effort), you may want to enable automatic updates from the software manufacturer.

However, due to the large number of computers that get automatic updates, it may take many days before your machine is updated.

Another concern is that if your machine has been turned off when an update tried to download, your machine may not get updated right away when you turn it back on. So even if automatic updates are turned on, go to the software website every two weeks to manually check for and download updates.

Reinstall your operating system, if necessary

In some cases, viruses and other intruders are just too crafty for software to catch and totally remove. The only cure may be to reformat your computer to wipe out all the programs and data on your disk and then reinstall your operating system. This should get rid of virtually all viruses or spyware that have been too persistent to remove any other way. Hopefully, you'll have a good, clean, current backup already on hand of the data you've created to reinstall on the cleansed device.

UAC Slider

If you use Windows, there are "User Account Control" (UAC) settings to help prevent malicious programs (malware) from damaging a system. UAC can help stop the automatic installation of unauthorized applications and inadvertent changes to system settings. Although you can change the UAC settings or disable them, be very cautious about reducing the UAC protection setting.

*****

Consider Getting a Low-Cost, Dedicated Internet Computer

Computer prices have come way down to a few hundred dollars for a basic computer. Consider having a separate "search-the-Web computer" that does not have any of your sensitive files on it. Then if this Web computer gets infected or taken over by hackers, you have less at risk.

Have a fast-enough computer

This may be the most overlooked item on anyone's security checklist. To keep your computer protected, you need to regularly use antivirus and antispyware programs to check and safeguard your computer's contents. Since running these programs is very intensive work for your computer and can take time, you don't want a computer that is so slow it discourages you from running these safety checks.

*****

USB Drives

Since plugging a USB drive (aka a flash drive) into a computer may pick up malware, you'll want to arm your USB with some antispyware and antivirus software programs that don't take up too much space on the drive.

Disable Autorun

The "Autorun" feature on USB drives, CDs and DVDs automatically opens up files when the media are inserted into a drive. By disabling Autorun, you can prevent malicious code on an infected USB drive from opening automatically.

Turn your USB drive into a stealth drive

If you're traveling light and just bringing along a portable USB drive with essential files rather than your laptop, be aware that plugging these drives into someone else's computer has the risk of leaving traces of your data and Internet activities on the host computer. Look for USB drives or software specially designed to prevent this from happening.

Security risks to your computer

On the other side of the coin, be aware that anyone who connects up a USB drive, MP3 player, PC card, Wi-Fi, Bluetooth, Firewire or Thunderbolt device to your computer may get complete access to (and make a complete copy of) your computer's contents if safeguards aren't in place. (Such access and copying is called "pod-slurping.")

*****

Administrator (Root) Mode

Depending on your computer's operating system and how you start your computer, you may be making a big mistake. Fortunately, you can fix this mistake if you read on.

Three ways to turn on a computer

There are three main ways to turn on a computer. By turning on the power, you may be giving unlimited (administrator, administrative or root) access, limited (standard) access or guest access. You can adjust your computer's settings to set the level of access.

You must have at least one administrator account on your computer so overall control is maintained. Be sure to give that account a complex, secure password.

What is an administrator account? An administrator account can go anywhere and do anything on your computer including install new programs (selected by you or a hacker who gains access to this account).

By contrast, a limited, standard account or a guest account can't *install* programs. A standard account can *run* programs, surf the Internet and create files.

With unlimited administrator access, you (and/or a hacker) has total control of every program and file on the computer. If you encounter malware, you are much better off with exposing limited privileges, not administrative privileges. Consequently, *use the administrator mode with total privileges only when necessary.* Remember, an administrator account is like having the master key to every office in a building.

Operating systems handle it differently

Your device's operating system may have you using the administrator account by default. In other cases, it may be disabled by default where you can enable it, as needed. Check to see if your device's administrator account is the one you're using right now when you turn on the device.

Depending on the operating system of your device, you may be able to set up a *supervised* account for your children where you can not only keep track of what they're doing on the Internet but also block websites in real time.

How to run as a Windows Standard User without losing your current account settings

If you've already been running your computer as an administrator and you want to start using a more protected standard-user account, you can maintain access to the files you've already created by first creating a second administrator account with password protection and then converting your original administrator account to a standard account. You would then use the standard account each day and provide the administrator password only when needed.

Older versions of Windows also have a guest account option that allows even less access to your device's vitals by others.

*****

Attachments

A very common way to infect your computer or other device is by downloading infected files attached to emails or messages. That's why you need to be especially careful when it comes to downloads.

If you're not positive who sent you a file or whether it makes sense for that person to send you a particular or suspicious attachment, don't download it. If it's someone you know, contact them to verify it's their attachment.

As soon as you download a file and *before* you open it, run a scan of the file with your antivirus program. Make this a habit for *every* file you download.

It only takes one infected download to ruin your day, week or life.

*****

Backups

Since disaster can take many forms—fire, flood, theft or a virus—having a backup of your data in the same physical location may not be enough. Look into also having an online backup service that automatically backs up your data offsite.

It's best to do regular backups after doing antivirus and antispyware scans first to get rid of any malware on the device. If your device later gets hacked, you'll be very thankful for having a good, clean backup.

*****

Recovery Disk

A "recovery disk" is a great insurance policy at little or no cost. It allows you to reinstall your device's operating system and initial software as it shipped with the device. This disk can be very useful if malware has infected your device and you want to restore your device to its pristine, original state. You can either get a recovery disk from the device manufacturer or create one on your own. Use your operating system's or antivirus program's emergency-disk preparation feature to create the disk.

You want to create your own recovery disk *before* there is any problem.

After you use your recovery disk, be sure to update all the software on the device.

Depending on how you create the disk, you may be either reinstalling software as it originally was on the device at the time of manufacture or the most current versions of the software.

You'll also want to have an offsite backup of your computer's contents in the cloud.

Another alternative, with a Mac, is using Time Machine which will provide a backup on an external disk of your current files and programs.

*****

Firewalls

Firewalls are a very important part of your protection when you venture out on the Internet. There are software firewalls and hardware firewalls. You want both types. Software firewalls are covered here. For information on hardware firewalls, see the next item, Routers.

Make sure your firewall is turned on even if you have a Mac. You can go into System Preferences and then Security and Privacy to get it turned on.

Use one software firewall at a time

A software firewall can help control what goes in and comes out of your computer. How many software firewalls are enough? One. With more than one software-firewall program turned on at one time, the programs may conflict with one another.

You may want to use the software-firewall program built into your device's operating system or get a specialized software-firewall program.

Always have a software firewall turned on

If you download a software firewall over the Internet to take over the firewall chores from the one in your operating system, be sure to have your operating system's firewall program turned on during the time you download the more robust software firewall so your computer is not left unprotected.

Also, whenever you turn on your computer, keep your modem cord unplugged from your computer and your wireless connection off (and/or don't start your Internet browser) until you look to see and verify that your software firewall loaded up.

Warning on allowing programs access to the Internet

Part of your software firewall's job description includes stopping dangerous programs and malware from accessing your computer. Sometimes, the firewall will ask you whether to permit access to your computer. If you don't recognize the name of a program asking permission to access the Internet, don't answer immediately. Instead, type in the program name in Google (www.google.com) to see if you can determine whether it is a legitimate program. If you're in doubt, just say no.

Don't be so quick to turn off your software firewall for tech support

There may be times when your computer isn't running quite right and a technical support person for one of your software programs will tell you that the problem must be a conflict between the software program and your software firewall. You may then be encouraged to turn off your software firewall to do some troubleshooting, which can extend over quite a period of time.

Be wary of turning off your software firewall while you're connected to the Internet. In many cases, it's something else that's causing the problem, not a firewall conflict. If you do turn off your firewall, you may be making your computer a sitting duck for malware.

If you decide to allow tech support testing and turn off a software firewall program that isn't part of your operating system, then at least reactivate the firewall that came with your operating system (e.g., the Windows firewall) so you have something in place to protect your computer during the troubleshooting process.

*****

Leak Testing

There are tools to identify leaks and available ports that could make your computer system and information vulnerable to hacking.

LeakTest is a free testing program to determine whether your firewall is working. Gibson Research Corp., https://www.grc.com/lt/leaktest.htm

ShieldsUP! is a quick, popular, free Internet security checkup and information service. Gibson Research Corp., https://www.grc.com/intro.htm

*****

Routers

Routers do more than allow several computers to access the same Internet connection simultaneously; they can also provide protection for your computer against viruses, worms and other malware.

On the other hand, routers have become a favorite target of hackers so read on to see how to better protect your router.

Install a router with a built-in hardware firewall

If this lingo makes you feel lost already, stick around. This is important information and you'll get the gist of it in just a few paragraphs. A router is a piece of hardware and your computer's modem gets plugged into it.

A router that's part of your Internet connection acts just like a high fence that's around your home. Just like a fence, it can make it more difficult for a stranger to see what's behind the barrier (e.g., your computer) and to go after what's being protected.

Some fences are more protective than others and some do a better job of completely concealing what's hidden behind the fence. Routers with built-in hardware firewalls are like that, too.

Although a router is ordinarily used with a computer network to connect up several computers to the Internet, you can (and should) use a router with even one computer.

Here's why. Every computer uses an address known as an IP (Internet Protocol) address to connect to the Internet. A router with built-in NAT (Network Address Translation) helps hide the IP address of your computer and that makes it tougher or impossible for hackers to find your computer. Outsiders see the IP address of your router, but not the IP addresses of the computers connected to the router. It's like a burglar looking on a map for your house but your house number is not listed.

As discussed above, you'll also want to have a software firewall, too. Some software firewalls help control not only incoming traffic to your computer but outgoing traffic, too.

Make sure you keep your "human firewall" turned on, too, by staying vigilant and careful.

It is worth the money to get professional help to set up a more secure wireless network especially if the following recommendations are foreign to you:

- Change the network name.

  Change the name of your wireless network rather than using a default name familiar to hackers.

- Change the factory-default router password.

  The wireless router password is different from the wireless network password. Change the factory-default router password to maintain control over your router; otherwise, a hacker who can find your router may be able to get control of it by typing in the factory-installed password and then doing a router rooter job on your computer.

- Update router software.

  Make sure your router software is kept up to date. If possible, have updates install automatically. One problem is that many router manufacturers don't keep their software up to date.

- Disable remote control of your router.

If your router's settings allow remote management, your computer could be attacked. Disable the remote management setting unless this is absolutely needed.

- Make your wireless router more secure.

  Routers can be hard-wired or wireless. Wired connections are generally more secure than wireless connections.

  Many wireless routers come with no security features automatically activated; the default setting often leaves your computer defenseless. Newer routers may make it easier to secure your network and Internet connections.

- Activate the highest security settings for your wireless network.

  These are probably the most protective steps you can take. If you have a wireless network, activate the highest security settings at every access point.

  There are several security standards. "WPA" security is more protective than "WEP" security and "WPA2" is more protective than WPA in encrypting data. There are different versions of WPA2. The most secure at this time is WPA2-PSK (AES). Avoid WEP—it's not secure.

- Use MAC address filtering.

  A router with built-in "MAC address filtering" can help restrict access by letting you specify and restrict the list of devices approved to be on your network. Make sure your devices are on the list so you don't get locked out.

  To some degree MAC address filtering can help prevent neighbors and strangers from piggybacking (using your network). Be aware, however, that a hacker with sniffer software can discover authorized MAC addresses (that's why you want to take the more protective steps of activating the highest security settings and using a secure passphrase).

- Have a secure passphrase.

  Use a "passphrase" (i.e., password) to access your network that's not easy for others to discover. A longer phrase with upper and lower-case characters and special symbols (e.g., $, !) will make it more difficult for bad guys to decipher your passphrase. The passphrase is typed (or copied and pasted) into each device on the network just one time, not each time you use the Internet.

  As with any password, put it on a written list that you keep in a secure place.

- Use Stateful Packet Inspection.

  For a more secure firewall architecture, use a router that has "Stateful Packet Inspection."

- Have a VPN endpoint router.

  Some routers have a built-in VPN endpoint that makes it easier to set up a VPN.

- Think twice before using the router from your Internet Service Provider (ISP).

  The router your ISP provides to you has the advantages of allowing remote updating of software and solving connection issues. But the advantages also increase the chance that a hacker might remotely gain access to your router. You may be better off buying your own non-ISP router.

- Maybe have a guest account on your router.

  Rather than give a guest total access to your router through your administrator account, set up a guest account with a guest password that is different from your administrator password.

  If you don't ever have any guests using your Wi-Fi network, then disable the guest account so it can't be used by strangers.

- Do your research.

  Research your router by looking up customer comments and reviews on its security.

- Turning it off can be great security.

  If you won't need your router for an extended period of time, turn it off.

- Routers may now be used by the police to solve crimes because routers may capture unique identifiers from devices and tie someone's use of the router to their presence at a crime scene.

*****

Restore Point, Rollback Software and System Restore

Your device may allow you to set a "restore point" that restores your device's programs back to what they were at a previous time. If changes (or malware) have caused a problem, a restore point gives you the option to reset your device's settings to an earlier point in time. The best time to create a restore point is once you've done a virus and spyware scan and found your device is clean. You might name the restore point as "Clean date [and put in the date of the scans]."

It's also a good idea to set a restore point before installing a new program so if things go south, you can go back to the restore point when your device worked correctly.

By the way, if your restore points are disappearing, that's a pretty good sign there's malware on your device.

A "rollback" software program lets you go back in time to undo more of the harm done to your computer. If you have the Apple OS, Time Machine can reset your system to how it looked on a prior day.

Depending on the level of infection of your device, using a restore point may not be enough. You may have to wipe your device clean and restore it to its factory-default status ("system restore") to get rid of the malware.
If you don't have a current backup in hand to restore your files, hopefully you've been using an online backup service so you can restore prior versions of files.

*****

Spyware

How do you know if there is spyware on your computer?

If any of the following are happening, there's a good chance you have spyware on your computer:

- You type in the name of a website and you are sent to an entirely different unrelated one.

- A search engine you *didn't* select is doing the searching.

- A toolbar appears that you haven't seen before.

- Random messages appear on your computer's screen.
- Your computer slows down.
- Certain keys no longer work in your Internet browser (e.g., you can't tab from field to field in a form).
- You see endless pop-up windows.
- New icons appear in the task tray at the bottom of your screen.

How can you prevent spyware from installing on your computer?

- Don't follow email links claiming to offer antispyware software.
- Don't click on links within pop-up windows.
- Close the dialog box when asked unexpected questions.
- Be wary of free downloadables.
- Adjust your browser preferences to limit pop-up windows.
- Keep your computer updated and regularly use antivirus and antispyware programs.

*****

Antivirus Programs

Many people feel antivirus programs are your best protection on the Internet. That's not true. The first and best level of protection is practicing safe habits (e.g., keeping all your software up to date and being very careful when visiting websites, downloading files or software and clicking on links).

The second level is having good hardware and software firewalls. The third level is having a good backup of your data.

An antivirus program is your fourth level of protection. Your operating system may come with a built-in antivirus program or you can install and activate one (but *not* more than one) antivirus software program; otherwise, conflicts may arise in the operation of the antivirus programs. For more protection, run your antivirus program in safe mode—that's a way to start your computer for troubleshooting.

Rather than using a standalone antivirus program, you may want to have one that is part of a security suite that also includes an antispyware program, software firewall and spam filtering.

You'll want to have one antivirus program, one antispam program, one pop-up blocker (unless it's already included in your browser) and several antispyware programs. Every week scan your computer using your antivirus and antispyware programs

Some programs also have a secure browser for financial transactions and virtual keyboards to stop keylogging (someone remotely recording your keystrokes, including passwords).

If you're using Windows, you may also want to use the free Microsoft Safety Scanner found at http://www.microsoft.com/security/scanner/en-us/default.aspx

*****

Antispyware Programs

Spyware is a computer program that tries to gather information about you or takes over your computer without your knowledge or consent for advertising, marketing or malicious purposes.

One less malevolent example is "tracking cookies," which track and record your movements on the Internet. Other spyware may involve pop-up ads on your device. Malicious spyware, such as Trojan horses, may record your keystrokes (e.g., the passwords you type in), destroy or capture your data, delete programs on your computer or allow someone to remotely control your computer.

Unlike antivirus programs, it is fine to install several antispyware programs and run them at least once a week. If your program has real-time antispyware monitoring (and it should), keep that feature turned on.

*****

Security Suites

You can get standalone products that offer antivirus, antispam, firewall and possibly other privacy protection such as a password manager. Another approach is to get a "security suite" that combines all of these products.

*****

Antispam Programs

Spam is unwanted email. Antispam programs can help prevent spam emails from arriving in your email inbox. Besides wasting your time, a spam email may contain malware or a link that activates malware when clicked.

Check your spam filter or folder at least weekly in case "real" emails are in there.

Reduce spam

Since spam is not only a time waster but a possible source of malware, you'll want to take the following steps to reduce the amount of your spam:

- Include a spam-prevention service as an add-on to your email program (which probably already has a spam filter).

- Set up and use a disposable email address that simply forwards emails to your actual email address to keep your actual address private.

- Don't open spam emails.

- Don't respond to a spam message by writing "Stop writing me" because all that does is validate your email address for the spammer.

- Similarly, ignore spam email removal buttons or links because clicking them just verifies the correctness of your email address to the spammer.

- Make the email address on your websites a little harder to be used by a spammer by replacing the @ symbol with the word "at" and replacing the period before the "com," "net", "org" or whatever extension you use with the word "period."

- Send group emails as a bcc (blind carbon copy) to hide email addresses, thereby reducing spam in case a spammer receives a forwarded email, too.

*****

Remote Control and Access

You should limit remote access or control of your computing devices. Check your devices' settings to see whether remote control is turned on; it should be turned off.

*****

Encryption

Encryption is a way to make information unreadable to anyone who doesn't have an encryption key to decode the contents. You can encrypt computers, tablets, phones, specific files, folders, entire disks and emails. It is more common for phones to come with excellent encryption but you can't always be assured that the encryption will be 100% effective.

Encryption is important because even if your device is password protected, there are ways to read unencrypted files on your device without knowing your password. Your device may have encryption built in as an option but require you to turn it on.

You may have read stories of unencrypted information being stolen from companies where much grief and financial loss could have been avoided if encryption had been used.

Encryption may be very important if you deal with highly sensitive or confidential information on your devices. Even with encryption, in general, you shouldn't have any of the following on your devices: Social Security number, driver's license number, birth date, mother's maiden name or financial account information.

Encryption features may come with your operating system or you may decide to use a third-party encryption program. Although encryption programs can keep outsiders from reading your files, these programs may slow down device performance.

Turn encryption on

For some apps such as messaging apps that have added encryption, you need to turn it on.

Encryption certificate and recovery key

Note that the first time you encrypt a folder or file, an "encryption certificate" is automatically created. You should back up your encryption certificate.

Save your "recovery key" in a safe place so you're not locked out of your own device. If your certificate and key are lost or damaged and you don't have a backup, you won't be able to use the files that you have encrypted. Note that if you use Windows 10 and use its default device encryption, the recovery key is not stored on your USB drive; instead, it is stored in your Microsoft's OneDrive cloud account.

Encrypt your email and signature, if necessary

Although most email isn't encrypted, there are encryption programs with varying levels of security and methods to encrypt emails and the email authentication process.

Some email programs have an add-on program that encrypts email.

Other email programs encrypt email but require both the sender and the recipient to have the same program to decrypt email messages.

The electronic or digital signature can be another valuable security tool. It tells the recipient who signed the document and that nothing was changed. The electronic signature is a typical feature of encryption programs. However, be aware that nothing is foolproof; electronic signature encryption has been cracked by hackers from time to time.

*****

Tracking software

Consider getting software that can track your computer's location and delete files remotely in case the device falls into someone else's hands.

*****

Deleting, Erasing, Shredding and Wiping

There are different ways to remove information from your computer and other devices and some are more permanent and destructive than others.

If you want to keep some or all of the information, be sure to not only make a backup but also test that the backup was successful before wiping out data on the device.

Deleted information can often be very simply undeleted. For example, emptying the Recycle Bin on a Windows computer does not get rid of files and data—they can be recovered unless more extensive steps are taken.

The best way to get rid of data and files is to first encrypt the entire drive with the encryption built into your operating system and then wipe out the data (repeatedly) with the utility that came with the drive or a program designed for that purpose. For added security, see if the program replaces all data with just zeros or random information. Repeat the process several times and then safely, physically destroy and dispose of the device.

Also, even if you destroy files and information, anyone you've sent this information to or who has stored it may still have the data.

One other step you might take if your computer becomes infected with malware is to reformat it to reset it to its factory condition. That not only destroys the files you created, it also reinstalls the device's operating system to the state it was in when it was brand new. Make sure you've backed up the data you've created *before* doing a reset.

Hard drives

There are different techniques and programs for destroying the data on a hard disk depending on the version of the operating system you're using and type of hard disk in your device.

There are two types of drives in computers—HDDs (hard drives) and SSDs (solid-state drives). SSD drives work differently. For them, encrypt the file and then see if the drive manufacturer has a drive-wide secure erase.

Smartphones and tablets

Generally, "factory reset" will erase data and files on a smartphone or tablet. The commands differ depending on the operating system used (iOS, Android or Windows).

It is more protective if you take an extra step of adding dummy data (with no metadata that is traceable to you) to overwrite any traces of your real data multiple times (at least seven). Better yet, repeat this factory-reset process several times and end with a final reset.

You want to eliminate all types of data—contact lists, phone calls, messages, emails, photos and even GPS information on where you live, work and go.

Some other ideas

Before you donate, sell or otherwise dispose of a computer, tablet, cellphone or other device, make sure you've followed the manufacturer's recommendation for permanently wiping information including files, Internet search history, contact lists, photos, calls made and received, voicemails and messages sent and received. Remove the sim card from your mobile device. Consider getting specialized software to wipe devices clean.

*****

Desktop Search Programs

There are security issues with desktop search programs.

A desktop search program allows you to quickly search for virtually anything on your computer. This type of instant search program may also allow anyone else to discover your information if they can get access to your computer in person or online (such as via hacking) for even a few seconds.

Because these search programs are instant finding programs, a search on your computer for "Social Security Number," for example, could quickly turn up every place it appears on your computer's hard disk.

To help prevent problems, have password protection or more sophisticated authentication procedures in place to operate your computer.

Maintaining privacy with shared computers

With some desktop search programs, if users use separate accounts (different usernames to log in), there are privacy options to encrypt the index so one user won't be able to access another user's desktop search index. You may also be able to limit access to specified folders.

Warning on multiple computer searching

If you're using one of the desktop search programs that can also search across multiple computers, you might want to keep this multi-computer search feature turned off entirely or at least specify that certain sensitive files or folders (including specific email folders) are not to be shared among the computers.

These programs may have separate consumer and enterprise (business) versions. Only the enterprise version may give management tools to centrally control whether the multiple computer search feature is turned on or off on each linked computer.

Be aware, too, the search-engine company may copy and store your data (for a limited or possibly an indefinite period of time) on the search engine's servers. Whenever a copy of your data is in the hands of someone else for any period of time, the chances of that data being used, released, hacked or subpoenaed go up.

*****

File Sharing

Limit your file sharing

Your computer may be on a home or work network where files or folders are shared. See which ones really need to be shared. The reason to restrict unnecessary file and folder sharing is that if one computer on your network gets infected, you want to ensure that the rest of the computers on the network don't catch the bug.

Homegroups

Computers can share (or not share) folders on a network.

A "homegroup" makes it easier to share files and printers on a home network. You can share pictures, music, videos, documents, and printers with other people in your homegroup.

Other people can't change the files that you share unless you give them permission to do so.

When you set up a computer with Windows 10, a homegroup is created automatically if one doesn't already exist on your home network. If a homegroup already exists, you can join it. After you create or join a homegroup, you can select the libraries that you want to share. You can prevent specific files or folders from being shared, and you can share additional libraries later. You can help protect your homegroup with a password which you can change at any time.

P2P file sharing

If you participate in peer-to-peer (P2P) file sharing where friends and/or strangers are sharing music or other files, you may be inadvertently allowing others to copy all your files and folders—not just the ones you wanted to share—and exposing your device to malware.

Some P2P applications have you open certain ports on your firewall to transmit files. Those open ports can give hackers access to your device. In addition, shared files may violate copyright laws or contain pirated or pornographic material, any of which could lead to legal prosecution and liability.

Remove metadata before sharing files

A word processing, spreadsheet or presentation file you create may contain "metadata" (hidden information) that you may not want to share when you email someone a file or provide a CD, DVD or disk. This metadata is not immediately apparent when you view the document. Metadata in a document can include:

1. Your name and the names of previous document authors

2. Your company's name

3. The name of your computer and the network server or hard disk where the file was saved

4. The location of the file on your computer

5. Document revisions and versions

6. Template information

7. Hidden text or cells and nonvisible portions of embedded OLE objects

8. Comments

Risks and embarrassments with metadata

What's the problem with distributing a spreadsheet, word processing, presentation or other file to customers, clients or coworkers containing metadata that hasn't been removed?

Computer-savvy recipients will be able to see the hidden data in your files.

So, for example, if you are "recycling" a document, agreement or presentation from a prior client for a new client, your new client may not only discover the old client's name and information that's hidden in the new document but also see what was modified (or wasn't) and how much (or little) work was involved in preparing the revised document. Revealing such information is not what you intended to happen and may also violate confidentiality obligations toward the old client.

Metadata removal

There are products that can permanently remove the hidden metadata.

Metadata cover-up is not removal

And if you really intend to delete metadata, make sure you don't just cover it up. For example, on documents converted from a Word file into a PDF, techniques such as covering text with black (putting black boxes on top of digital text) or adding graphics on top of existing graphics don't hide or delete what you want removed.

If you share files and/or images, you need to know what metadata is and how to remove it before you start sharing. Metadata may differ depending on the type of file.

Metadata in photos

By default, most social-networking sites do not share GPS (location) and other metadata with images you upload to their sites. However, this information is captured by the service itself unless you disable location services on your camera/phone. If you already have photos that contain GPS data, there are programs that can strip out that information.

*****

Macro Security

A macro is a computer instruction that performs a series of computer instructions. Some viruses hide in macros in computer files.

Go to the macro settings in your software programs and tighten up your macro security.

*****

Printers and Copiers

Often overlooked are some copiers and multifunction printers that have a hard drive, operating system and a networked connection—just like computers; therefore, they need secure passwords and security features. One security feature is to encrypt connections to and from your computer on a network.

Another security feature is to encrypt an administrator password via an https connection when the password is sent from a computer to a printer.

Data thieves are increasingly targeting such equipment since they can be easy to hack into as documents are being sent from a computer to the printer.

If your printer allows people to send print jobs over the Internet such as through "FTP" (File Transfer Protocol) print jobs or IPP (Internet Printing Protocol), consider disabling this feature if you don't need it. If your computer uses SNMP or the stronger SNMPv3, change the default SNMP community name to a strong password.

If malware infects a printer, it could affect all the computers on the same network, too.

Keeping printer software and drivers up to date is important also to prevent security breaches.

Since your printer may be an all-in-one printer with a hard drive that stores print jobs, faxes and what has been scanned or copied, there's a risk of losing or exposing that data if the printer is stolen, traded in or given away. You need to erase data you don't want others to see. It may be possible to attach the drive to your computer to use erasing software.

Depending on the type of copier you have, the same issues may be present.

6. Protecting Phone, Mobile Device and Camera Security

Mobile Devices

Mobile devices have virtually the same security issues as computers. The problem is three-fold.

First, mobile devices such as smartphones and tablets may be storing sensitive data such as credit-card numbers, digital wallets and online purchase accounts and contact information, and these devices can connect to the Internet.

Second, mobile-device security attacks are more common now than ever before. Make sure you're familiar with your device's security controls and choose the most restrictive settings. In addition, apps are a way hackers can cause trouble for you so make sure you look at reviews and privacy policies before you buy or download; get apps you can trust.

Finally, some mobile devices may have fewer built-in security features than computers and/or the ones that are present often are not turned on.

*****

Cellphones

Your life may be on your cellphone. It may contain your emails, messages, contacts, photos and other sensitive and/or financial information.

Smart cellphones and tablets are, in essence, computers. That means they can be infected by malware, just like computers, and that malware can do the same type of damage or even more.

You owe it to yourself to make your cellphone as secure as possible by taking the following steps:

- Lock your cellphone with a strong, unique, complex password or passcode to help prevent someone else from accessing your information if your phone is lost, stolen or momentarily left unattended.

- Consider using your fingerprint instead of a password.

- Avoid using automatic log-ins to email accounts where no one has to type in a password.

- Have your phone automatically lock out and require a password if the phone is inactive for a certain period of time.

- Read the fine print of the permissions you're giving before downloading an app—you are probably surrendering more information about yourself than you realize.

- Be very careful using banking and financial websites and make sure the URL starts out with https:// rather than just http—the extra "s," as in security, is important.

- Limit your use of public Wi-Fi since it is not as secure as your phone provider's network. See Hotspots in Chapter 9.

- Don't "jail break" your phone to allow unscreened apps that may contain malware to be downloaded to it. (For more on jail-breaking, see Apps below.)

- Use antispyware and antivirus software (and keep them up to date) to prevent malware from getting on your phone; one type of malware can even remotely turn on the cellphone's built-in camera and microphone.

- Enable or install a phone finder or tracker on your phone in case it's lost or stolen and file a police report, too. See if your phone has built-in software that gives you the ability to remotely delete all data on your phone and to lock it down if the phone becomes lost or stolen; if your phone doesn't have such built-in software, see if you can obtain it elsewhere. If your phone is lost or stolen, contact your phone provider right away.

- Decide whether to let all callers, just your contacts or no one see your Caller ID.

- Be aware your cellphone is beaming your location unless that feature is turned off.

- Be aware photos you take (and post) may contain your location data, too, unless the geotagging feature is disabled.

- Regularly back up your data, photos and other items in case you lose your phone or it becomes infected with malware.

- Pay attention to your cellphone's call log and emails—your phone may be infected if you see calls or emails you don't recognize.

- To prevent advertisers from getting more information about you, go to settings to limit ad tracking (or to turn personalized ads to the "off" position).

Disposing of your old phone

If you trade in, donate or discard your cellphone, your data will still be on it unless you follow the instructions in your cellphone's manual to wipe it clean.

*****

Apps

Apps can be great. They can also be invasive as far as your privacy and security.

Before you install an app

Before you install an app, take a moment to look at the terms and conditions to see what information it wants from you and who has access to that information.

App creators may be asking for permission to access your contacts, calendar and location, learn which websites you visit, view your messages and emails, upload your photos and more. All of the accessed information may be used by the app maker and/or sold to third parties for marketing or other purposes.

Apple has an extensive approval process for apps for its devices that are sold through the Apple Store. With a Mac, for example, under Security & Privacy, you can only allow apps downloaded from (1) Mac App Store, (2) Mac App Store and identified developers or (3) Anywhere.

Apple's Gatekeeper built into some versions of Apple software can help protect your Mac from apps that could adversely affect it—but it is not foolproof.

Google is now requiring developers of Chrome extensions to inform you of the information they collect.

Jail-breaking and rooting

"Jail-breaking" allows a phone to run apps that aren't approved for the phone. (It's called "rooting" with Android platforms.) Such apps may not have gone through an approval process. Jail-breaking can be risky with unauthorized apps and may also void your phone warranty.

Extra decision on apps with passwords and PINs

With shopping, banking and other financial accounts, you'll probably have a choice between having passwords and possibly PIN information stored in the app or having you enter it each time you want to use the app. Whatever is stored can be stolen. You need to balance convenience vs. security.

Unlink or uninstall unused apps

If you're no longer using an app, there is no point allowing it to continue to collect information on you. If you used a social media account to log into the app, you can log into that account to unlink or delete it.

*****

Lost or Stolen Phones and Computers

Cellphones

Mobile devices used for work are especially attractive to thieves because it's easier to steal a laptop or other mobile device than it is to hack a database.

While you still have your phone, write down your phone's serial number. You can find it stamped on your phone or you can probably get it from the Settings option on your phone.

If you can't find your phone, take these steps before you panic:

- Call your phone to see if it's close by.

- If you don't have a phone to make the call because your phone is missing, send an e-mail to yourself using the hashtag #lostphone in the subject or body and the app IFTTT will call your phone, helping you find it. See https://ifttt.com/recipes/1828-help-me-find-my-lost-phone

- Use the Find My Phone app for an iPhone (http://www.apple.com/support/icloud/find-my-iphone-ipad-ipod-mac/) or for Android phones, go to https://support.google.com/accounts/answer/6160491?hl=en

- There are also apps that can show you where your device is on a map and send you an email with its location.

- If you still can't find your phone, contact your phone carrier to put your phone on a blacklist to prevent it from being reactivated in the U.S. Also get instructions on remotely erasing all information on the phone and resetting it to factory-default settings.

Kill switch

If your cellphone is lost or stolen, you'll want to contact your cellphone provider and also remotely activate a kill switch (if one is on your phone) to disable the phone.

A kill switch isn't perfect because some criminals are able to impersonate you (as the true owner of the phone) to get the phone revived.

By the way, there is tracking utility software that can track your lost or stolen computer and phone home to let you know the location of the device.

Backups

Whether it's a phone or a computer, having a good, up-to-date backup is essential in case your device is ever lost or stolen.

*****

Protecting Your Phone Privacy

- Have an unlisted phone number so conventional telephone directories don't list your number.

  There are other kinds of directories (criss-cross and reverse directories) that are organized by address or phone number and also show a person's name. Even with an unlisted number, your information may appear in these other directories.

  To request removal from a leading criss-cross directory, contact Haines & Company at 1.800.843.8452.

  There are many directories and information-broker websites but you'll probably never get removed from all of them.

- Register your personal residential phone number with the National Do Not Call Registry at https://www.donotcall.gov or 1.888.382.1222.

  This can help reduce the number of telemarketing calls but note that even if you register with the service, you may still receive political calls, charity calls, survey calls and business-to-business calls.

- To avoid being contacted, don't include your phone number (or your email address), if possible, on your voter registration form. If your local registrar of voters already has either or both of these items, you can re-register to vote and omit that information.

- Don't include your name or phone number on your outgoing voice-mail/answering-machine message.

- If you get a phone call (including a call from someone who called your number by mistake) asking what your phone number is, don't reveal it; instead, ask the caller what number they are trying to dial.

- Use "call blocking" to block your phone number when making calls.

  You can either block on a per-call basis (by dialing *67 before dialing a number) or on a per-line basis (i.e., all the time when making calls). If you have permanent per-line call blocking on your phone and you want to display your number when making a particular call, just dial *82 before dialing the number.

- You can also hide your phone number by using a service such as Babble.ly which turns your phone number into a Web link; people see the Web link and not your phone number. The website makes the call for you. Calls are limited to 10 minutes.

- Skype and Google Voice are another alternative.

- Make sure you have a good password on your account with your cellphone company.

- Screen who is calling you by having Caller ID on your phone lines for incoming calls (your cellphone has this and you can add it to your landline either for an extra monthly fee or as part of a phone-line package).

  Note that your Caller ID will not show the caller's correct phone number if the caller is using "spoofing" to have a false number displayed.

- A "Call Screening" feature will let specified callers hear an announcement that you aren't available and your phone won't ring on these calls.

- "Anonymous Call Rejection" (ACR) lets you see who's calling before answering the phone. Your phone won't ring if the caller has a blocked number. The caller has to call back and unblock their phone number for your phone to ring.

- For the most anonymous calling, use a pre-paid calling card (paid for in cash) from a pay phone.

Speakerphone issues

Your phones may be sending radio signals even when you're not using them. As a result, some cellphones and hardwired phones can be microphones picking up and sending out your conversations when the phone isn't being used but you're talking nearby.

What to do with old phones

Your cellphone may have your calling, messaging and email data as well as your contact lists. Landline phones can retain a record of incoming and outgoing calls.

Before you donate, sell or dispose of your old phones, look at the phone manuals for the necessary steps to remove your data.

Telephone records

If someone has access to your telephone records, they have access to the details of your life.

Your calls and records can tell someone about your friends, family, business associates, doctors, pharmacy, daily routine and vacations as well.

Since there are websites that sell cellphone records, see whether your cellphone company will permanently remove your call details from your cellphone bill.

Cell towers and stingrays

Some local, state and federal agencies have put devices called "stingrays" in aircraft that emulate cell towers to track the location of criminals' cellphones.

In addition, local law-enforcement agencies have small, handheld cellphone-tracking (finding) equipment that might not require court orders under federal laws.

*****

Charging and Recharging Your Devices

Hackers are always looking for ways to gain access to devices. Even so ordinary a task as recharging your device may provide that access depending on where you do the recharging.

- Be aware that you take some risk using a charging kiosk or recharging station at an airport terminal or a shared computer at a library. (Hackers call this "juice-jacking"). It's safer to just use a regular outlet plug at those locations.

- Even using a USB cable to connect up to a friend's infected computer or a shared, library computer can allow malware to be put on your device.

*****

Cordless Phones

Cordless phones may not be as secure as you think.

Your cordless phone may use the same 2.4GHz microwaves as Wi-Fi. Although your Wi-Fi transmissions can be encrypted, your cordless phone may or may not be encrypted. It depends on what is built into the phone.

If you have an older, analog cordless phone, it is easier for people to eavesdrop on your conversations. Newer digital phones offer more protection with encryption. They also offer the ability to set digital security codes (change the factory-default code setting) and, in some cases, a new digital code every time the cordless handset is put in the base charging unit.

Encryption

You'll probably want a phone with DDS or better yet with DECT (often referred to as "Wi-Fi friendly") that has some encryption. Another alternative is using VoIP (Voice-over-Internet Protocol) that has built-in encryption.

However, with any cordless phone, there is still the possibility of someone with a radio scanner listening in to your phone conversations. Consequently, you probably shouldn't discuss sensitive personal or financial information on a cordless phone.

*****

VoIP

"VoIP" (Voice over Internet protocol) is also known as "IP telephony." It allows you to use the Internet to make telephone calls.

Whenever you hear the word Internet, think about security. Go through the VoIP security settings so they are correct for you. Also make sure you keep your VoIP software up to date.

Encryption may be the default or an option with VoIP—it's a good idea to utilize it. And, of course, use a firewall as well as antivirus and antispyware software.

If security goes awry, a hacker could take control of your phone, make fraudulent calls or eavesdrop on you.

Your VoIP provider may hide your IP address to help protect your computer from hacker attacks.

*****

Mobile Wallet Payments

Many merchants accept mobile payments from your cellphone or other device. Since payment protections should carry over from the type of payment used, it is safer in general to use a credit card rather than a debit card as the source of payment for your mobile wallet.

Mobile payment procedures differ. Some mobile payment procedures store in your device the last four digits of your credit card and your transaction history—others are more secure and don't store any credit-card or transaction history.

Some mobile payment providers assert that their security features are stronger than those with credit cards because the credit-card information is encrypted, not stored on a phone and not shared with merchants.

Depending on which system you use, there may be more security by requiring the use of a PIN or fingerprint to unlock the wallet and/or creating a unique token or code for each transaction. It's also a good idea for you to have a password and two-factor authentication on your phone.

Finally, use an app that generates instant electronic receipts, which you can check immediately and also later reconcile with charges on monthly statements.

There are special risks with mobile payments including the following:

- Your information is more widely exposed with mobile payments than with traditional payment systems since the app's payment mechanism as well as the merchant's may be involved. As a result, select a secure payment app.

- Treat your device with the same degree of care as you would your purse or wallet. Just as you make them inaccessible, lock your device with a unique password.

*****

Cameras

There are two types of cameras that can invade your privacy—ones that look at you and ones that you wear.

Your computer or other mobile device probably has a camera. Be aware that malware out there can remotely turn on the camera (and microphone) on your computer or other device without your permission. That could be embarrassing or worse if your device is in your bedroom. So here's a tip: cover up your computer's or tablet's camera when it's not in use (you can attach a small, Post-It Note over the lens).

Wearable cameras present a different issue. Besides invading the privacy of others, they can generate a biometric movement pattern as you walk, run or climb that could identify you through a computer algorithm.

Another issue is "geotagging" where a geographic location is added to a photo or video.

Webcams

Webcams, sometimes referred to as "IP cameras" or "Internet Protocol Cameras" are digital video cameras connected to the Internet. Some hackers can remotely start up the webcam on your computer, baby monitor or other device. Play it safe and cover up your webcam camera.

And as with any device that connects up to the Internet, change the default passwords on the device to a strong, unique password. Yes, webcams can have passwords, too.

Some TVs have built-in webcams for video chatting and they may be vulnerable, too.

*****

Geotagging and Photographs

Geotagging is the process by which geographical identification metadata (usually latitude and longitude) is added to various media such as a geotagged photograph or video, website or SMS message.

As a result, strangers who see you in photos or videos may discover where you (and/or your friends and family) live, work or hang out. If you post enough photos, a criminal could track your movements and know your daily schedule.

Fortunately, you should be able to disable the geotagging function on your smartphone or camera, edit the photo or video to strip it out or turn off the geotagging function on the photosharing site you use (it may be turned off by default).

*****

Location Tracking

There are three main ways your movements can be tracked.

First, by carrying a cellphone everywhere and keeping it on all the time, you are broadcasting your location when you go to sleep, when you wake up and where you are in between.

Second, when you click OK to an app's privacy agreements and terms of conditions, you may be giving up a lot of your privacy (including location tracking) to those corporations and the companies they sell your information to. In some cases, apps track your location even when you're not using them.

Third, photos may reveal where the photos were taken (see Geotagging above).

Your physical location information can be shared not just with your phone provider but also with other apps on your smartphone, too.

Depending on the operating system on your smartphone, you may be able to see which apps are or can be tracking you.

*****

Photo Vaults

Also known as "ghost apps," "photo vaults" are apps that allow people to conceal photos, video, text messages, phone calls and other often sensitive information in plain view on their cellphone.

7. Smart Homes, TVs, Cars and the Internet of Things

Smart Homes

You may have a dumb home, a smart home or a combination. No matter what type of home you have, you need to secure it.

There's more to protecting your home than locking all of your doors and windows.

Living with a smart home

You may have a smart digital home connected to the Internet. When you see or hear the word "Internet," you know that security issues are present, too. Malware could open your garage door, change thermostat settings or start sending malicious emails through your devices.

You want protective software that can not only block known threats but also has the ability to recognize malicious signatures of unknown threats as well as determine when a device is not operating properly. Be aware that protective software is never 100% effective.

Protective software for smart-home devices can either be one product that covers all your smart devices or separate software for each device.

Since your smart-home devices are connected to a router to access the Internet, make sure your router is fully protected by strong WPA2 administrative controls, strong router passwords and router software that's kept up to date. Make sure your Wi-Fi router can notify you if any other devices log into your system.

Keep your devices from spying on you

Many of these smart-home devices are voice-activated, which means there's a built-in microphone that's ready to record you at any time.

Those conversations may be sent to third-party marketing companies to use in advertising and marketing. Or if hackers get hold of them from those companies, those recordings could be used for purposes you really wouldn't like.

Could a smart scale end up sending your weight changes to your employer or insurance company?

Your home may be too smart for *your* own good. You may have a smart digital home where your garage doors, thermostats and more are connected to the Internet.

Remember, if you have your garage door hooked up to your wireless network, it will be easier for you (and others) to open up the garage with a smartphone (and perhaps have easy entry into your home from the garage).

What makes it tougher to protect yourself with the IoT (Internet of Things) is that there is no consensus for networking standards. That makes it more difficult to prevent vulnerabilities for the applications in your smart home.

Your front door

If you have a peephole on your front door, make sure it has a wide angle viewer so a stranger can't hide from you.

So you don't open your door to strangers, consider having a camera installed at your front door at a high enough height to prevent removal.

There are also smart doorbells that come with a video camera. One advantage of these is that you can chat with visitors to your home using the Internet so the visitors don't know that you're not home. Videos of the visitors can be saved online for future review, if needed.

Motion detectors that turn on lights can be useful, too. Another possible feature is a motion detector that notifies you if someone is there and they don't press the doorbell.

Other "dumb" home steps

Locks on gates are a must, too. Keep shrubbery cut back so burglars can't hide while breaking in. Dogs can be useful protectors, too.

It's a good idea to see identification before letting repair people in.

Eavesdropper-proof wallpaper

If you're really worried about criminals capturing your electronic transmissions, there's a new material that may turn your home into a Faraday Cage similar to what the military uses for secret communications (think Get Smart's cone of silence).

Don't have a dumb home

Don't turn your smart home into a dumb home. Keep your financial and sensitive personal records at home in a safe place where roommates or workers who come into your residence can't access those records.

What to do when you buy or sell a smart home

If you sell a smart home and leave behind any Internet-connected smart devices such as a garage door opener, alarm system, security camera, thermostat, refrigerator, washer, dryer or water-drip system, the buyer may have access to your living habits and information (think security cameras) that's stored in the cloud.

On the other hand, unless you or the buyer make changes to the passwords, access codes and usernames, the seller may have access to the buyer's living habits and more.

For a good list of steps to take on the transfer of a smart home, look at The Smart Home Checklist at: https://otalliance.org/system/files/files/initiative/documents/ota_smarthome_check_list.pdf

*****

Smart TVs

Your TV may be listening to (and recording) more than just your commands to change the channel or to search for a program. That built-in microphone may also be picking up all your conversations in front of the TV. Some TVs have built-in webcams for video chatting and they may be vulnerable, too.

Your TV may be in your living room, den or bedroom so be aware that what happens in front of your TV (or its built-in webcam) may not stay with your TV or in your home.

Third-party companies are often used by manufacturers of smart TVs to convert your speech into text so they could have access to your voice recordings.

Consequently, if unneeded or unwanted, see if you can disable voice commands (or set up voice commands that are triggered or activated only when a button on the remote is pressed).

See if using your TV's Internet features or your digital, video recorder box company requires you to allow sharing of your viewing habits. Your "anonymized" information may allow companies to identify your viewing habits. See whether this "sharing" feature is turned on or off by default and learn how to turn it off.

Other steps you can take

Realizing most smart TVs usually don't have the best security features, you may want to discontinue using the smart part of your smart TV for privacy reasons.

If you don't want to use a smart TV's Internet features, don't connect the TV to the Internet via Wi-Fi or hard-wired Ethernet.

If you've already connected your TV to your Wi-Fi network and want to discontinue it, see whether you can delete the Wi-Fi password, or better yet, reset your TV to the factory-default settings—just make sure you don't again provide the Wi-Fi password after resetting your TV.

If you *do* want to use Internet features, you may be more secure not connecting your TV directly to the Internet. Instead, you may want to connect your TV to another device (e.g., gaming console, digital-player set-top box, etc.) that's connected to the Internet. Remember you'll still need to deal with the fact that these other devices may have their own security issues and also keep track of and report back your viewing habits.

*****

Game Consoles

Some game consoles which are attached to your TV can see what you're doing and listen to you while the TV is on. Look for a setting to turn off those controls.

*****

Virtual Reality Devices

Take a look at the terms and conditions (t&c) before you use the virtual reality device. The t&c may allow information to be collected on you (what is being watched, when it is used and your head movements) and sent to several companies.

*****

Smart Cars and Car Rentals

Cars are now highway computers with up 20 million lines of computer code (more than some airplanes) so there are many ways hackers can use cars to intrude on your privacy and security. Favorite entry points include Wi-Fi, Bluetooth and keyless locks.

Unfortunately, cars don't have the same password and encryption protection present in financial accounts. As a result, whether it's your own car or a rental car, you need to be aware of the following:

- You may create a big risk if you program in your exact home address in the built-in GPS. A car thief, valet or future owner of your car could see where you live. Couple that knowledge with an integrated garage opener and you risk exposing your home address and a way to get into your home.

  To reduce this risk, program in an address a few blocks away but not your exact address. (Don't put in another home on your street because the bad guy might drive down your street trying the remote on every home.) Putting in a nearby address is a good idea for your phone's GPS, too.

- Use a valet key rather than your full-privileged car key (or remote fob) when letting others have access to your car. Also, be sure to have your car registration paperwork in a locked glove compartment that your valet key can't open. Also be sure to only hand over the valet key and none of your other keys (e.g., your house key).

- Your car may have an integrated remote control that is paired up with your garage door opener, gates or locks. If that's the case, before you transfer or trade in your car, check the manual to see how to reset your garage door opener, gates or locks to prevent anyone else from having an easy way to get into your garage (and maybe your home).

- If you use the car's built-in Bluetooth or a USB device to connect your smartphone to the car and use its features (e.g., make calls, get directions, etc.), the car is storing your information. The next car owner or renter may have access to your address book and contacts unless you take steps to erase them.

  If you connect up your car to your social-network services and apps and store your searches, events, etc., in your car's system, you'll need to take steps to delete the information in the car. It's also a good idea to log into your social networks and delete your car's infotainment system's privileges.

  There's no one way to erase this information. It varies by car model. You want to access the command to erase user data or, better yet, revert the system to a factory default reset. Check your car's manual or ask the car manufacturer for the best way to protect your information.

- For more privacy, rather than using a car's built-in Bluetooth system, buy and use a third-party Bluetooth kit. See Bluetooth in Chapter 9.

- To charge your phone, use the cigarette lighter rather than a car's USB port.

- Many cars now have a built-in GPS device which transmits your vehicle's location to a centralized service.

- Many cars have black boxes (or use cellphone apps) that track a lot of information about driving. (This field of technology is known as "telematics.") In addition, car insurance companies are trying to get consumers to voluntarily have devices installed to track their driving habits. There is a risk that this data could be divulged if a subpoena were received by the car insurance company.

- There are apps to turn your post-1996 car into an Internet-connected car using a port under the steering wheel.

- There is now a gadget that can capture the wireless-key command to open most new cars (and your garage and alarm system) without your knowing that there is a problem. The only clue is that it takes two tries for your key fob to work. There are bags that can block the radio signals coming from a car key fob.

- Security researchers have discovered how to remotely manipulate many car controls. For example, hackers could use the entertainment system to gain control of and shut down the braking system. That's why malware protection is being developed for cars.

- If you're really worried about carjackers or burglars who might follow you home, get a humble-looking used car. Willie Sutton, the legendary bank robber was asked why he robbed banks. He answered, "Because that's where the money is."

- Make sure your car gets all necessary updates to protect the software in the car.

8. Traveling

Traveling Tips

Here are some tips if you're traveling:

- Boarding passes have more information on them than you can see. The barcodes have personal information on them that can be easily read with readily available barcode readers. This information could allow someone access to airline information about you. Besides using this information for non-flight purposes, someone could change or cancel your flights. For these reasons, don't post photos of your boarding pass online and do shred them after a flight.

- The tag on your luggage may have your name, home address, phone number and/or email address. You may not want other people to know that you're away from home. For that reason, either cover up the tag or use a tag when the flap folds down.

- Have an inexpensive laptop or tablet that you only use for traveling.

  Only place essential files on the device that you'll absolutely need while traveling and try to avoid including financial and sensitive personal files.

- Use encryption and a VPN to connect to the Internet. Log out of the device if you won't be using it even for a short period of time.

- On the road, make your laptop computer more inconspicuous by using a backpack rather than a laptop case to carry it.

- Carry onto a plane your electronics such as phones, tablets and computers. (If you're traveling internationally, make sure the electronics are charged up and can be turned on for airport security inspectors to avoid having them confiscated.)

- Take only essential paper files. If you need to shred them or other materials while on the road, make sure to use a cross-cut (or micro) shredder.

- When you make a reservation and check in, just use your first initial and your last name. If the hotel check-in clerk announces your room number in a loud voice, consider getting another room.

- Use a hotel safe for valuables which can include your electronic equipment.

- Cover your room front door peephole with a Post-It Note or bandaid.

- Clean out your wallet/purse before you leave on a trip and only take what you really need. Limit the number of credit, debit and ATM cards you take with you.

- Don't take checks unless absolutely needed.

- Don't take your bills with you.

- Make sure newspapers don't pile up while you're away.

- Have the Post Office hold your business and personal mail.

- Be aware that hotel business centers have public computers that are more risky to use since keyloggers and other malicious software may be on them.

- Be careful what you say and what you read and type while in public areas. Useful for traveling, a privacy filter for your monitor prevents fellow passengers on a plane or train from seeing what's on your computer screen. Some manufacturers are building privacy screens into their laptops that can be turned on and off by pressing a button.

- Decide whether to use an "Out of Office" auto-reply on your home or work accounts that advertise you're away (and your home or office may be unoccupied). Some employers are instructing employees not to include "out-of-office" replies in their emails that can tell hackers when computers are unattended.

- Some employers request that employees not post vacation photos while they're away to prevent the theft of a work laptop left at home.

9. Wireless and Wireless Networks

See Chapter 5 for additional protective steps.

Hotspots

Keep from getting burned at hotspots

You may use a wireless (e.g., Wi-Fi) connection at a hotspot (e.g., coffee shop, hotel or airplane) or even a wired network connection (e.g., at some hotels) to connect to the Internet. Some hotspots have better security protection than others. Be aware that even wired connections can be "sniffable" where sniffer software can penetrate the defenses of the network. Therefore, as a first line of defense, try to minimize your use of hotspots, especially if you're dealing with sensitive information.

Evil twins

These are illegitimate wireless networks that appear to be trusted Wi-Fi connections to the Internet. Here's how this scam works: an attacker positions himself by a Wi-Fi access point such as a coffee shop and broadcasts his own imposter signal (as the evil twin) to get you to log on to his network and reveal your passwords, credit-card numbers and other personal information.

Protective steps you can take

- Make sure your firewall is on to protect you.
- Avoid downloading software updates at hotspots since it may be malware and not a real update.
- Make sure your Wi-Fi settings don't allow your device to automatically connect with the nearest Wi-Fi access point.
- When not in use, turn off your wireless card.

Email at hotspots

If you're not using a VPN (Virtual Private Network), both your email login password and your emails may be vulnerable at hotspots unless you use some kind of secure connection.

When you check email at a hotspot, you're either using a Web-based account (e.g., Google's Gmail) or an email program that's on your device.

Web-based account

If you use a Web account to handle email, you can have a more secure login to protect your password by going to a login Web page that starts out as https:// rather than as http://. The "s" stands for "secure." Using a secure site to log in for your email keeps your password safer. However, you may then be redirected to a regular http site to read and send emails.

Find out whether you automatically stay on a secure site after logging in to protect the privacy of your email reading and sending. If not, see whether you can take steps to get more complete protection.

Email program

If you're using an email program that's on your device to check email at a hotspot with your ISP (Internet Service Provider), rather than the hotspot's ISP, see whether your ISP or email program offers a secure connection for checking email (secure POP3 or secure IMAP) or sending it (secure STMP).

However, if you must use the hotspot's ISP to connect to the Internet, it may not be that secure.

That's where a Web-based email service such as the secure connection for Gmail discussed above may be the safer way to go at a hotspot if you don't use a VPN (see below).

Instant messaging

Try not to use instant messaging at hotspots since this is not the most secure method of communicating.

Wi-Fi vs. Cellphone provider network

You'll have more security using a cellphone provider's network than a Wi-Fi connection especially if your service automatically logs you into an available *public* Wi-Fi network when you're in range.

*****

VPN (Virtual Private Network)

The most protective step you can take at hotspots is to use a VPN (Virtual Private Network).

A VPN scrambles what you do on the Internet by creating a secure, encrypted private tunnel when using the Internet. It can offer security similar to an https site, which can help protect not only your email (check for compatibility with your email program) but also all your other Web traffic. A VPN can be useful even with a wired, home connection that's not on a network.

If you're connecting to a corporate network, also use a VPN so your connection is more secure.

If possible, see if your VPN is cross-platform so it can work not only with your computer but also with your tablet and cellphone. Also find out if the VPN provider keeps data logs on users.

See if your router has a built-in endpoint to make it easier to set up a VPN.

A VPN is generally more secure than using an SSH tunnel, although both are useful for encrypting Internet traffic.

*****

Bluetooth

Bluetooth is the standard short-range wireless interconnection of cellphones, computers and other electronic devices.

Bluetooth generally has a broadcast range of up to around 30 feet. But the range can be up to 300 feet or sometimes extended up to a mile depending on the device you're using and the equipment a hacker has on hand.

For Bluetooth devices to communicate, they need to first pair with one another. The pairing process occurs not only when a secure connection is established but also when devices are most vulnerable.

You can put your Bluetooth-enabled device in "discoverable" (visible) mode or "nondiscoverable" (invisible or hidden) mode.

When your device is set to discoverable mode, it is available to pair up with other Bluetooth devices and transmit data back and forth. If a hacker detects a discoverable signal, he can attempt to pair with your device and hack in to steal (or later regenerate) the PIN (Personal Identification Number code, also sometimes called a "passkey") without your knowledge.

Even if your device is in nondiscoverable mode, it is still discoverable to any previously paired device—that's a good reason not to accept pairing requests from unknown senders.

The pairing process starts with one user entering a PIN, which is used to generate a link key. This initial exchange between devices occurs over an unencrypted link so it's vulnerable. The link key can be stored in the device's memory to authenticate and authorize the devices when they connect up again in the future. Once devices are paired, they have full access to the shared services on the other device.

The dangers of Bluetooth

There are six main ways a hacker can attack your Bluetooth device:

1. By "bluebugging," hackers can eavesdrop on your telephone conversations as well as make calls, send and receive text messages and access the Internet on your phone. Some mobile devices are susceptible to bluebugging but not bluesnarfing (see next item).

2. Through "bluesnarfing," hackers may be able to access your mobile device's data (including contact information) without your knowledge. Generally, newer devices block bluesnarfing.

3. With "bluejacking," business cards are sent anonymously to your Bluetooth device trying to get you to add the sending device to your address book. Don't do it. If your device is set to a nondiscoverable mode, bluejackers shouldn't be able to find you.

4. "Bluesniping" is when a hacker uses a laptop and a powerful antenna to extend the broadcast range.

5. Mobile viruses can spread via Bluetooth to your devices. Your mobile device could then transmit a virus to your computer via synchronization.

6. With more cars using Bluetooth, a hacker can use software to send and receive audio from a Bluetooth connection in your car.

Although certain versions of Bluetooth offer more protection, none is perfect.

19 Ways to Better Protect Yourself When Using Bluetooth

1. Lower your presence by keeping Bluetooth turned off when you're not using it. That includes turning off your headset when not being used.

2. In general, when Bluetooth is on, keep your device in the nondiscoverable (hidden) mode rather than the visible mode. Read the Bluetooth portion of your device's manual so you know how to make your device invisible and turn Bluetooth off.

3. Since devices in discoverable mode often have a default name, change the name to something anonymous.

4. Once paired, go to nondiscoverable mode. This invisibility will not affect that pairing.

5. Pair devices in private.

6. If devices become unpaired in public, go to a private location to pair them again.

7. Don't pair with unknown users or devices.

8. Don't accept files from unknown or suspicious senders.

9. Periodically look on your device at the stored list of paired devices to make sure only invited devices are included.

10. Use a long, complex and not easily guessed Personal Identification Number (PIN) code when pairing devices. PINs are four or more character alphanumeric codes. A total of eight to 16 letters and numbers is recommended. The longer the PIN, the harder it is to crack. Some devices are manufactured with only a four-character limit, which is very vulnerable.

11. Change default passwords for wireless headsets.

12. Use built-in security features that only let authorized devices (e.g., your mobile device and your computer) communicate with one another.

13. Use encryption when connecting with a computer.

14. Use combination keys as link keys rather than unit keys for better security.

15. Install antivirus software on your mobile devices.

16. Periodically check the device manufacturer's website for security patches and updates.

17. Don't store sensitive data such as credit card numbers, your Social Security number or passwords on any wireless device.

18. If you lose your Bluetooth device or it's stolen, make sure the previously paired devices unpair your device so the lost or stolen device can't access the services of the paired devices that are within the broadcast range.

19. Avoid using Bluetooth during meetings. Bluetooth is sometimes used to create a temporary computer network during meetings so files can be shared among computer users. Because there is no built-in security with this type of sharing arrangement, someone out of sight but within range (potentially up to 300 feet away or more) could link up with the networked computers to capture data.

The best advice is avoid using Bluetooth in very public settings such as airports and trains and use the invisibility and other security settings whenever possible.

*****

Wireless Networks

Change your wireless network name and make it invisible

Hackers are aware of the default SSIDs (public network names) of wireless networks and routers. To help prevent problems, take four steps.

First, change the network name. Don't use your name or other identifying information in naming the network.
Second, disable broadcasting the name by turning off or changing the setting to "invisible" so your router is kept in more of a stealth mode.

Third, you can go a step further and change the router's IP (Internet Protocol) address setting to make it more difficult to find your router.

Fourth, disable remote management of the router unless absolutely needed.

For more tips on securing your wireless network, see http://www.onguardonline.gov/articles/0013-securing-your-wireless-network

Don't overbroadcast your signal

Restrict the strength of your wireless network's signal. The stronger your wireless signal, the greater the likelihood that outsiders can tap into it. Adjust the signal strength so it's just enough to reach each access point and no more. Locate access points in central locations away from windows and outside walls.

Don't accidentally broadcast wirelessly

If you're not using this function (e.g., you use hard-wired Ethernet cables to connect up computers), disable the wireless features so you don't accidentally start broadcasting wirelessly.

How can you test whether your Wi-Fi network is secure? If you're using Apple's OS X, see whether there's a padlock icon by the network name. With Windows computers, look for your network's name and you'll be secure if you see the words "Security: WPA2" or "Security: WPA2-PSK" next to the network name.

There's a special reason to be concerned if your wireless network is not secure. Some criminals use unsecured Wi-Fi networks of unsuspecting consumers and businesses to help cover their tracks in cyberspace.

Failing to secure a wireless network can allow anyone with a Wi-Fi-enabled computer within about 200 feet or so (even someone driving by—"war driving") to tap into your Internet connection.

Activate the highest security settings for your wireless network so you don't face the task of proving to legal authorities that you had nothing to do with criminal activities using your home or business network connection.

Wireless extenders

If you install a wireless extender to improve coverage, be sure to secure it with a password.

Piggybacking

"Piggybacking" is where you use someone else's Wi-Fi network or someone uses yours.

10. Internet Safety

Also see Firewalls and Routers in Chapter 5 and Hotspots and VPN in Chapter 9.

Internet Risks and Solutions

Every Internet-connected activity creates its own security issues such as someone:

- Stealing your financial information and files
- Altering your files
- Stealing your passwords
- Using your computer for illegal activities
- Using your computer to attack other computers

Anonymity on the Internet

When you visit a website, certain information can be automatically sent to the site that may include:

- The browser you're using and your device's operating system
- The websites you visit
- The search engine you used to get to the site
- Your computer's unique IP (Internet protocol) address
- Your passwords and files if you're on a malicious site

Lower your profile and risks

When it comes to protecting yourself and your information, your first line of defense is finding ways to make yourself, if not invisible, at least harder to see and find.

Consider getting a low-cost, dedicated Internet computer

Consider having a separate "search-the-Web computer" that does not have any of your sensitive files on it. Then if this Web computer gets infected or taken over by hackers, you have less at risk.

Don't be connected all the time

If you have an always-there, always-on connection to the Internet such as through DSL or a cable modem, you're increasing the chance that someone will find your connection and attack it. Unlike dial-up connections where your computer's Internet (IP) address changes with each call, with an always-on broadband connection your computer's IP address changes less frequently, if at all.

So it may be smarter to disconnect your high-speed modem or wireless connection when you're not on the Internet or better yet, just turn off your computer or tablet when you're away from it.

Make your social-networking settings more private

- The people most interested in your postings may be identity thieves, corporations and debt collectors—not your friends and family.

  Decide what you want to be public knowledge vs. private knowledge about you.

- Determine whether you want to use an alias or no name at all to protect your privacy.

That comment or photo you posted just for friends may end up all over the Internet. Your information may be reused in ways that you have little or no control over.

- Think twice (or three times) before posting your age, address, phone numbers, email addresses, date of birth, city of birth, names of family members, vacation plans and photos.

- See what information is public by default (and can be changed to private) and what is required to be public.

Set up your Internet security and privacy levels

Your Internet browser generally lets you select the level of security and privacy you want to have while you're surfing the Internet.

Firewalls

There are software and hardware firewalls to keep bad guys out. A router with a hardware firewall can help you have anonymity on the Internet but it's not enough to hide. Your devices need to have software to prevent attacks and counteract them if hackers get through your defenses.

Pharming

"Pharming" is where a fraudulent website contains copies of pages from a legitimate website to capture your confidential information.

Phishing

"Phishing" is when "phishers" send you an email that looks like it's coming from a known company or person with a link to what looks like a legitimate company site. It isn't. It's a fake site designed to get you to divulge personal and sensitive financial information. To ensure legitimacy, some bank sites have an image and phrase you preselect on their websites that come up each time you log on to the correct site so you know the site isn't fraudulent. "Vishing" is the same type of scam through phone calls.

"Social phishing" is where someone poses as your friend using information you've posted on the Web, often at social-networking websites.

Spear phishing

Phishing that's targeted for certain individuals (usually within companies) rather than just anyone is known as "spear phishing."

Don't click on links

The way to have phishers go home empty-handed is to avoid clicking on any link in any email or IM. Instead look up the correct Web address on Google or some other search engine and type in the URL (the Web address) of the site yourself.

Toolbars

Before installing a toolbar, search on the Internet to see if the toolbar creates problems that outweigh the benefits. Be careful because toolbars are sometime bundled with other software.

Truncated URLs

It is more and more common to receive links to a website or an article with a "truncated" (shortened) "URL" (Web address).

These shortened URLs don't reveal exactly where you're going. You may be in for a nasty surprise when you arrive at the website. To prevent this, you may want to use a program that expands the URL before you click on it.

AutoComplete

The AutoComplete feature can save you time. It can also cause problems. You may end up sending an email to the wrong person if you click the wrong person on the AutoComplete list.

If you use AutoComplete, always take a second to double check the correctness of what has been completed. Also delete email addresses on the AutoComplete list that you don't send to anymore to reduce the chance of error. You may decide to turn off the AutoComplete feature.

Automatic Sign-Ins

If you sign into one of a company's services and stay signed in (e.g. Gmail), you may be allowing the company to accumulate information on you as you use all of the company's services such as email, Internet searches, watched videos, etc.

For example, each time you sign in to your Google account, make sure the "Stay signed in" option isn't selected to reduce the amount of information collected on you.

You can disable automatic sign-ins.

EULA

An End User Legal Agreement (EULA) is a legal agreement between the manufacturer and purchaser of software that spells out the terms of usage. A EULA must usually be accepted before a download of the software is allowed.

Most people do not read EULAs before accepting them even though the agreement may:

- Allow the vendor to monitor your device activity and share it with a third party, both of which could have privacy and security implications for you

- Allow the vendor to install additional software on your device

Privacy policies

You see (or probably ignore) privacy policies when you download apps; sign up for social networks, online services and websites; or receive them in the mail from banks, credit-card companies, insurance companies and more.

In some cases, if you opt out of the privacy policy, you won't be allowed to download the app. In other cases, you can still get the service and be able to restrict the sharing of your information.

It's important for you to take a look at privacy policies. For example, you may discover that the website does not guarantee that private information will remain private. Or you may discover that an app wants to know your location and contacts and have access to your messages and emails.

JavaScript

Using JavaScript on the Internet may expose you to malware. It is probably a good idea to uninstall or disable it.

Adobe Flash Player

Because using Adobe Flash Player while on the Internet is not as secure as it could be, your computer or device could be exposed to malware. Therefore, you may want to uninstall this program from your devices.

If you must use Flash, use the Chrome Internet browser that has Flash built in but sandboxed (kept separate).

Internet Service Providers

You connect to the Internet through an Internet Service Provider (ISP). It is becoming more common for ISPs to work with data brokers to track and accumulate information on customers.

*****

HTTPS

If you're dealing with banking, credit-card or other financial or sensitive information, just use websites that start out with "https." They are more secure than websites that start out with "http."

The "s" after http stands for "secure." A secure site is designed to encrypt your credit card or other data while traveling between your Internet browser and the website's server.

An *https* site should have a *lock icon* in a corner of your Internet browser (not on the Web page itself) with the lock in the closed position. Be aware that phishers sometime put a fake lock on a fake site. To test the authenticity of a lock, double left-click it to see the security certificate for the site. If no certificate appears, then it's definitely a phishing site. However, even if a certificate does appear, make sure the name of the site and the name under the Issued To tab on the certificate match one another. (Depending on the browser with your phone, you may not be able to view a certificate.)

Look for the lock before you send personal or financial information online.

Unfortunately, there's more to consider if you're not the trusting sort of person. Certificates may be *high assurance* (authenticated) or *low assurance* (unauthenticated). Many Internet browsers currently cannot distinguish between the two types and the lock icon looks the same on both types of sites. Some third-party programs/add-ons can distinguish between the two.

Also, in some cases, cookies can infect HTTP connections that are later transmitted for HTTPS connections.

There are several other protective steps you can take. First, you can just use a separate "Internet credit card" with a low credit limit for your online transactions. Second, either your credit card or PayPal account may allow you to use a one-time *virtual* credit-card number for a single transaction that is different from your credit-card number. Finally, you can use a VPN for a more secure connection.

By the end of 2016, the U.S. government is requiring the use of HTTPS on all public websites and web services.

*****

Online Shopping

With online shopping, only use websites that start out with "https."

Always print out the confirmation page and confirmation order of your online orders.

Other tips for online shopping

- If you type in a website URL, type carefully because malicious sites often have URLs close to the correct ones.
- Use one browser just for banking and shopping online and another browser for your other online activities.
- For more protection, use a credit card rather than a debit card. Consider using PayPal.
- Have a separate credit card for Internet orders.
- Don't send your credit-card details by email or enter them on an unsecured website.

- If possible, use a *single-use* credit card that's tied to your credit card but can only be used for one transaction.

- Think twice before allowing websites to permanently store your credit-card information (for future transactions).

- Don't use public Wi-Fi (e.g., libraries, hotels or airport computers) when making purchases.

- Use your cellphone data plan rather than Wi-Fi for online shopping.

- Use a VPN for more security.

- Log out of your account after making a purchase and delete cookies.

- Make sure the retailer is a legitimate business (check reviews outside of the retailer's website).

- Always match up charges on your credit-card statement with your receipts.

- Calendar the billing cycles for your statements and be sure to contact a creditor if a bill isn't received on time.

- All things being equal, it's probably safer to shop at companies located in the U.S.

- See if the company lists a phone number.

- See if there is a physical address shown for the business.

- Limit what personal information you give to merchants and never give out your Social Security number.

- On warranty registration cards, just provide your contact information (e.g., don't list income, age and other personal information).

- See if your employer prohibits you from using your work email address for online shopping sites.

*****

Cloud

Cloud computing, also known as "the cloud," refers to storage of your information not on your device but rather at offsite locations.

There are cloud backup services that allow you to store and retrieve large or unlimited amounts of information.

Determine what your needs are. You may just want your data backed up or you may want it synced across multiple devices so you can access the information anywhere where you have an Internet connection.

Currently, there is more legal protection for privacy of your information if it is just on your computer or other device as compared to being in the cloud in the hands of a third party.

Just as you need to protect the information that's on your devices, you also need to protect your information stored on the cloud. Neither can be 100% protected but certain steps can help:

- Use a strong, unique, complex password to access your cloud information from the cloud provider.

- Use two-factor authentication for access to information in the cloud if that's available.

- Decide whether sensitive information should even be uploaded to the cloud.

- Consider encrypting your information before uploading it to the cloud.

- Make sure the cloud provider uses strong encryption of your data—consider selecting a cloud site that uses the zero-knowledge approach where your data is encrypted before it reaches the cloud and only you hold the encryption key to decrypt it.

*****

Browsers

Just as with operating systems, Internet browsers (i.e., Firefox, Edge, Internet Explorer, Chrome, etc.) differ in their protective level.

Whichever browser you're using, check regularly to make sure you have the latest updates to minimize security breaches.

You can adjust the security settings in your browser. You may be at risk if you have Flash, JavaScript or ActiveX controls.

Some browsers have features or add-ons that provide additional security protection such as deleting flash cookies (supercookies).

Tor Browser

"Tor" is a computer network using free software for anonymous communication over the Internet. It helps to conceal a user's location and Internet usage (visiting websites, sending messages, online posts, etc.) provided you connect to websites with an HTTPS connection. Tor comes with an HTTPS Everywhere default add-on. There are reports that a hacking tool exists that can compromise the Tor anonymous browser.

Remember that anonymity does not mean protection against malware on the Internet. You still need to practice good Internet habits, keep your programs up to date, have protective software on your device and do regular malware scans.

Some people take things a step further on the road and also use a travel router that has been modified to anonymize all Internet traffic.

Pop-up blockers

You can change the setting in your Internet browser to block pop-up ads when you surf the Internet.

*****

Cookies and More

Apart from malware, there are three main ways your Internet movements and actions can be traced—through cookies, Flash cookies and beacons.

Cookies

A cookie is a block of text placed on your hard drive by a website when you visit the site. That cookie is then used to identify your computer the next time you access the site. It's a tracer on your hard drive that helps a website remember who you and your computer are.

Some cookies do more than this. They also track your movements on the Internet to give marketers a private profile of your interests. Sometimes online sites do it with your permission but some do it without your knowledge or permission. For example, with "clickjacking," ads are made invisible below cookie notification messages. When you click the message, you are actually clicking the ad and sent to the advertiser's website.

First-party and third-party cookies

There are "first-party cookies" and "third-party cookies." First-party cookies are used by the websites you visit. Third-party cookies are used by advertisers to track your online history and provide ads. Usually, you'll need to adjust the settings in your Internet browser (e.g., Chrome, Firefox, Internet Explorer, Edge or Safari) to block third-party cookies.

The cache is a folder that's a temporary storage area for pages and images you've visited. While you're in your browser, get rid of the files and cookies (stored in your cache) several times a day that you may unknowingly pick up when you surf the Net.

If you don't "clean the cache," your computer's performance can slow down and you're exposing your Internet browsing habits to more cookies. Different browsers have different menu options to perform the same housekeeping tasks; some tasks can be done automatically for you.

Cookie syncing (matching)

With "cookie syncing" (also known as "cookie matching"), websites merge databases of users' browsing history and increase the amount of information collected on you.

Public computers

If you're done using a public computer at a library or hotel, clear the browsing history (including cookies. log out of the browser and also restart the computer to minimize the information you've leaving on the computer.

Flash cookies (Supercookies)

Supercookies (also known as "local shared objects" or LSOs) are a special kind of cookie used on many sites. You get this type of super cookie by visiting a website that runs a Flash application and it contains a lot more information than a run-of-the-mill cookie.

They do have legitimate uses such as remembering your preferences for watching videos but they can also track you as you move from site to site. They can track you even when you're in private browsing mode. Because the usual process of clearing cookies in your browser doesn't clear out Flash cookies, you'll need a special add-on to your browser or a specific program to clear them out.

Evercookies

Evercookies come to life through "respawning" where cookies (such as Adobe Flash cookies) that have been deleted come back to life.

Beacons (aka web bugs)

Some websites use beacons to spy on you. Also known as *web bugs* or pixels, beacons keep track of what you're typing and doing on a Web page (including mouse movements).

There is software designed to blocks beacons. But before installing such software, check out the privacy policy and how the software might use your information! You don't want to solve one problem and create a new one in the process. Also look at customer reviews to see whether browser performance is affected by the beacon blocking software.

To avoid activating beacons, make sure your email program doesn't automatically download images from emails or read HTML.

*****

Fingerprints on the Internet

Real-world fingerprints are unique for every person. "Internet fingerprints" are unique for every computer, tablet and other device and show a device's unique set of hardware and software settings. Your Internet fingerprint can be collected when you visit websites.

Since Internet fingerprints don't leave a fingerprint on your device (you really don't know your device is being fingerprinted), fingerprints are replacing cookies as a way of tracking Internet usage in part because they are more difficult to block or remove.

You can make it harder to fingerprint your device by uninstalling or blocking JavaScript on your device. Some browsers have add-ons to block JavaScript. Note, however, without JavaScript, it may be more difficult to load videos or to function at all from many websites.

Test your device

If you go to https://panopticlick.eff.org/, you can see how unique your device is so you'll have some idea of how identifiable you are as you surf the Web.

*****

Householding

"Fingerprinting" tracks your Internet usage on a device. "Householding" fingerprints or tracks you across multiple devices you use.

*****

Cache

When you browse on the Internet, it's not only the websites that are trying to gather information on you. Your computer does it, too, through its cache.

The browsing data contained in your device's cache includes things such as your browsing and download history, stored passwords, certain cookies and more. You can delete some or all of this data for a specified period of time or forever through your Internet browser.

It's a good idea to clear your cache and browsing history several times a day because your browser's cache has information that an attacker could use to possibly exploit your online accounts or analyze your browsing history (and use the results to improve an attack on you).

*****

Search Engines and Your Security

Search engines may store your search history forever.

The good news is that your search history is generally tied to your computer but not to your name.

However, your name and search history can be linked together. How? If you use a search engine and also another service offered by that search engine company (e.g., email account, online groups or online photo storage), then the company may have your name, address and other kinds of personally identifiable information (PII) about you which they could link up with your search history. Is this 1984 or just part of modern-day life? You decide.

All of this collected information could possibly become available not only to hackers if they penetrated search-engine security defenses but also to the government and maybe even to litigants (e.g., via subpoenas in divorces).

DuckDuckGo is a search engine that emphasizes protecting the privacy of searchers. This is a search engine that says it doesn't collect information on you as you surf the Internet (https://duckduckgo.com). It's also already an option on some browsers (e.g., Firefox).

*****

Search Engines and Your Data

Virtually all of the search engines maintain databases that have your search history, which can include financial, medical, religious and other private information about you. If you do a search on your Social Security number and/or your name, you could be creating a problem. That search is part of the search engine's searching history, which you can't remove.

Websites you visit may know your computer because the site can see your unique IP address. There are a couple of ways to prevent this. If you use a service such as Tor (https://www.torproject.org), your IP address can be hidden.

Another approach is to use a VPN (Virtual Private Network). With a VPN, the websites see the VPN IP address, not yours. See http://lifehacker.com/5940565/why-you-should-start-using-a-vpn-and-how-to-choose-the-best-one-for-your-needs

Search engines retain your IP address for varying periods of time that may last more than a year. As previously noted, the search engine DuckDuckGo says that it doesn't collect your personal information at all.

Although information on your computer may be afforded more legal protection from litigation and government searches, that is not the case with your information on the servers of third parties.

Search-engine toolbars and free screensavers and games may be an avenue to provide more information about you or to install malicious software. Think twice before downloading one of these offerings.

*****

Private Browsing

Depending on which Internet browser you use, private browsing may not mean what you think.

In general, "private browsing" means your browsing activities aren't recorded on *your* computer—it does *not* mean that the websites you visit (or third-party companies they've contracted with for sharing information) or your ISP (Internet Service Provider) aren't collecting your information. All the main Web browsers (Firefox, Safari, Internet Explorer, Microsoft Edge, Chrome, etc.) allow you to turn on private browsing.

At this time, the Firefox browser is offering a beta version "stealth mode" to prevent third-party tracking (but not your ISP from tracking) when using the private mode.

Again, to have more privacy, clear your browser cache at least one or more times each day.

You can go a step further and use a Web-based proxy that sends your requests to see Web pages through another computer. With a proxy, neither your ISP nor the websites you're visiting will know the IP address of your computer.

If you're using a company computer, private browsing may not be so private because the computer may contain software to track your browsing habits.

*****

Do Not Track

In theory, with the Do Not Track feature, you can set your Web browser (i.e., Firefox, Safari, etc.) so your browsing behavior as you go from website to website is not shared with advertisers.

That's the theory. In practice, websites and advertisers may ignore it and track you anyway unless you install separate, protective anti-tracking software. "Do not track" features in some browsers only work if the websites you visit are set up to allow this blocking. Most sites don't allow the blocking.

The Federal Trade Commission (FTC) is working on a new Do Not Track rule. At the time this book is being written, it appears that the new rule would not cover companies that deliver information services to you (e.g., Internet search engines, browsers, phone companies, etc.).

*****

The Forget Button

For more control over your privacy with the Firefox browser, you can add a Forget button to the Firefox toolbar. Click it to wipe out browsing history from your selected time frame without affecting the rest of your information. For example, you could wipe out only your browsing history and cookies for the last 24 hours but keep every other time frame. See https://support.mozilla.org/en-US/kb/forget-button-quickly-delete-your-browsing-history

Private browsing

The Forget button is different from Firefox's Private Browsing which deletes your browsing history and cookies when you close the private window. With Private Browsing, you set it up in advance of your browsing. With the Forget button, you use it after you've done your browsing.

Private Internet searching

For more private Internet searching, Firefox offers the DuckDuckGo search engine as an option in the search bar's dropdown menu. DuckDuckGo does not keep track of your searches (unlike most search engines) and does not log IP addresses.

At the time this book is being written, Firefox is pre-beta testing a new tool to block browser tracking across sites.

*****

Online Dating

Online dating sites can be a great way for you to find your special significant other or unfortunately, for an identity thief to find *you*.

Your online profile may reveal your age, profession, income, education, religion, number of children or other details about your work and personal life.

By the way, when you look at other people's online-dating photos, right click them and look at the Properties menu to see the date of the photos.

*****

Blogging

As you would do with any social-networking site, be careful when you blog on your own website or someone else's. Only post what you'd want your current or future employer or significant other to see.

Determine whether you want everyone or only certain persons to see your blog posts.

Before you get started, find out whether any of your *private* information on the blogging website will be accessible by others.

You may want to take a few of these privacy protective steps as a blogger:

- Use *private registration* to hide your name, address and phone number when you register your own domain name; otherwise, people can look up the website in WHOIS and find out your address and phone number.

- Don't post personal information including your birth date, birth place, address, email address, phone number, Social Security number, driver's license number, school name or genealogical information.

- Consider using a pseudonym.

- Be careful broadcasting your current location or where you're going.

- To maximize your privacy when you post on your site or another's, you might want to use software like TOR to help hide the IP address of your device. Some websites note your IP (Internet Protocol) address that is unique to your device and can be used to identify you.

- Always delete all cookies after visiting a social-networking site and possibly also exit your browser.

- Before you comment on someone else's blog, see whether you can do it anonymously. Bear in mind that the blogging site may put a cookie on your device so it can see where else on the Internet you've gone (and what else you've posted).

- If you want more privacy and anonymity for your blog posts, consider using a "ping server."

- If you want more privacy by staying out of search engines, have a robots text file tell search engines to ignore your domain. For example, see https://support.google.com/webmasters/answer/6062596?hl=en

*****

Virtualization

If you're really adventuresome and have a techy gene or two, you might venture into the realm of running virtual machines. With virtual-machine software, you create a virtual (nonphysical) clone of your computer to venture out into the Internet. The original is safe and sound at home. If the clone gets infected out on the Internet, your main system is unaffected. You just get rid of the infected clone, create another copy and use the new clone.

*****

Dropping Off the Internet

You may fantasize or actually try to get yourself off the Internet. How would you do this (after first backing up vital information)?

- The first step would be removing your social-network presence from the Internet including Facebook, Twitter, LinkedIn and Google. If you can't end an account, you might change your information to something random.

- Your next step would be to try to remove your information from a search engine (e.g., Google, Bing and Yahoo). Google has a removal tool.

- If you've posted on websites or blogs, see if you can get your posts removed.

- Next, delete your online shopping and cloud storage accounts.

- If you've posted on websites or blogs, see if you can get your posts removed.

- Have your landline and cellphone companies remove your information.

- Contact the information-collecting websites such Spokeo and PeopleFinder. You might hire a service that specializes in removing your public information.

- Delete your email accounts.

11. Apple, Facebook, Google, Microsoft and Social Networking Apps and Sites

The Importance of Diversification

One very important way to protect your information is to use different companies for different services—Internet searches, social networking, email, TV, messaging and phone to prevent the accumulation of your information in one place with one company.

*****

Apple

Even with an Apple product, you need to deal with security issues.

Mac warning

With Macs capable of running Windows, all those Windows PC security issues you thought you could ignore as a Mac user could give you a big, unhappy surprise when you run Windows. Actually, smart Mac users need to take certain security steps even if they don't run Windows.

Passcodes and passwords

You use "passcodes" for your mobile devices and a "password" for your Mac.

You should set up a passcode for your iOS device (e.g., iPhone, iPod or iPod touch) to protect your data. Each time you turn on or wake up your device, use it to unlock it with your passcode.

Since so much of your life is on a device, don't choose the shortest possible passcode. Instead, have a longer one or a custom alphanumeric code.

If your device supports Touch ID, you can use your fingerprint instead of a passcode.

With the Mac OSX operating system, you can and should have a login password so your device is more secure. Have a complex, non-obvious password. (For more on passwords, see Chapter 3.)

Two-Factor Authentication

Two-factor authentication is an extra layer of security for your Apple ID designed to ensure that you're the only person who can access your account, even if someone knows your password.

With two-factor authentication, your account can only be accessed on devices you trust, like your iPhone, iPad, or Mac.

When you want to sign in to a new device for the first time, you'll need to provide two pieces of information—your password and the verification code that's automatically displayed on your trusted devices. By entering the code, you're verifying that you trust the new device.

For example, if you have an iPhone and are signing into your account for the first time on a newly purchased Mac, you'll be prompted to enter your password and the verification code that's automatically displayed on your iPhone.

Because your password alone is no longer enough to access your account, two-factor authentication dramatically improves the security of your Apple ID and all the personal information you store with Apple.

Once signed in, you won't be asked for a verification code on that device again unless you sign out completely, erase the device or need to change your password for security reasons. When you sign in on the Web, you can choose to trust your browser so you won't be asked for a verification code the next time you sign in from that computer.

Auto-Lock feature and previews

If you leave your phone around, you may want to have the Auto-Lock feature come on in a shorter period that you designate.

This feature prevents previews of emails and messages from showing up on your locked screen.

Expiration date

You may want to have iMessage, voice and video expire over time in case your phone falls into the wrong hands.

Recording your information

Technology companies gather and use your information to determine what your needs are and also to make money through advertising and marketing.

To assist you (and them), many tech companies want to learn about your regular activities, your search history, your contacts, your location, your apps (how long you use them and when you use them) and to some extent, your emails.

In general, Apple has indicated that it won't collect this information. Instead, the information will just stay on your phone. As to your search history and location, Apple's operating system (OS X) and its Internet browser (Safari) let you turn off the recording of that information and disable your frequently-visited locations.

You may not want to allow iPhone's location-based tracking by disabling various services. However, you'll probably want to keep the Find My iPhone setting in case your phone is lost or stolen.

It's not just Apple that would like to know your location at any given time; your apps probably do, too. If you want to be alerted when an app is tracking your location, you can have an icon displayed in the status bar showing when you're being tracked; simply change your Status Bar icon status.

On the other hand, Apple offers you privacy through encryption. Apple has stated that it can't access stored data (e.g. phone calls, text messages, photos, etc.) on newer iPhones if the phones are protected by a password, PIN or fingerprint and running the latest operating system. (Some Android phones are encrypted by default while on others, you need to enable it. In general, iPhones offer more protection at this time.)

*****

Facebook

Since so much of your life and information may be on Facebook, you'll want to review your Facebook account to have security and privacy protections in place.

There are two ways your information may be revealed on Facebook.

First, you'll be asked to supply information in response to items on Facebook's About page. That page asks about your work, education, places you've lived, your email address, websites, mobile phone, birth date, gender, who you're interested in, your political views, family members and relationships, details about you (your birth name, nickname) and life events. Limit what information you supply.

Second, Facebook allows you to adjust certain settings that increase or decrease who can see your information.

Have a strong unique password and change it over time

Have a strong, complex password and one that is unique to Facebook. Remember that passwords are not a one-time thing. It's a good idea to change your passwords at least every six months.

Consider using two-factor authentication (2FA)

If someone gets hold of your password, they can do a lot of mischief in your name. Consequently, you may want additional security with two-factor authentication (2FA) for logging in or in case someone tries to log into your account from a browser you don't use.

With 2FA, you get a text message on your cellphone with a code to enter for logging in.

If you're a high school or college reader of this book and have friends who may think it's funny to mess with your Facebook account, you may also want to set up "Login Notifications" on the Security Settings screen to get a text or email if a device or browser you haven't used tries to access your account.

Have a unique username for Facebook

To make it more difficult for someone to collect information about you across the Internet, use a unique username for Facebook so it doesn't match the one(s) you use on other social media. Pick a username that doesn't provide information about you (e.g., don't use your name or email address as your username).

Avoid links for logins

Rather than clicking on a link to Facebook in an email, go to the Facebook website to log in. Otherwise, that link may take you to a malicious site instead.

Avoid logging into websites with Facebook

If you use "Log in with Facebook" on a website, you are exposing more of your information. Instead, log in as a guest or anonymously if that option is available.

Adjust your general settings

Facebook, by default, wants everyone, including strangers, to be able to search for you in Facebook and see your name, user name, email address and phone number; send you messages; request to become your Friend; and even see your Friends list. You should change those defaults so access is available just to Friends or Friends of Friends rather than the entire public.

Having more security always involves the tradeoff of restricted access. You should restrict who can send you Friend requests and Facebook messages, look up your email address and phone number, see your future posts and see your Timeline and photos.

A good way to control who sees your information is to create a group and control your audience by selecting that group (e.g., to see your posts).

You can also customize your privacy settings to override default settings such as broadcasting your location.

If you want to see other Facebook accounts without divulging too much of your information, you can do so. When you create a new Facebook account, use your name but don't supply any other information, even a photo. Go through each of the settings and make them as private as possible choosing either "Only Me" or just "Friends" (and don't list any Friends).

How do others view you?

If you want to see how a particular person views your profile, click View as Specific Person (and enter the person's name in the window).

Restricting the information you provide

Keep in mind that Facebook requires you to use the name you use in real life in setting up your account—what your friends call you in real life or what your identification shows. (This is different from your username which was discussed above.) Restrict the information you provide on your profile. Think twice or three times before sharing your birthdate, phone number or address.

The most restrictive privacy setting lets the public only see your Facebook profile and cover photos, the people you're following, the groups you belong to and a link to contact you (which can be restricted to Friends of Friends).

Other information you shouldn't post

- Be careful with addresses whether giving the exact address or posting a photo that may be geotagged (and thus tied to a specific location).

- Posting information about your current or prior jobs can come back to bite you. And if someone wants to break into workplace computers, your Facebook page may be a source of entry.

Public Likes

If you like or comment on a post, anyone who can see the original post can see your activity and it is pushed to your Friends' feeds. So before you like or comment, first look to see if it is a public item (there will be a little globe icon). Also check on your Facebook Privacy Checkup settings to see with whom you're sharing your posts.

Whose messages can appear in your InBox?

Your choices are Basic or Strict.

Control who posts and also who sees your posts

You can limit access to your posts and who can post to your timeline.

This is very important because Facebook now allows all two trillion public posts to be searchable. What this means is that if you don't post to your Facebook Timeline as "Friends only," everyone can search for and see all your posts because they are public.

Restricting what Friends post on your timeline

It's one thing when you want to post on your Facebook timeline but it may be something else when your friends put items on your timeline. You may not be so happy with what they're posting.

You can adjust the settings so you can review posts and images you're tagged in before they appear on your Timeline.

Deleting your Facebook search history

Facebook keeps track of everything you've searched for using Facebook. You can delete some or all of your Facebook search history.

However, deleting your searches is not a one-time event. You can't tell Facebook *not* to continue recording your searches. You'll have to repeat the "delete search history" again…and again.

Unless you take certain steps, your Facebook search history is sitting there intact and includes who you've searched for, photos, posts, groups, etc. You can either select individual items to delete or your entire history.

Controlling the ads you see

You can control the ads you see per your ad preference settings.

Removing yourself from Facebook ads

There's another way ads may affect you. Based on your "likes" or "shares," you may be in them unless you opt out on the ADS tab.

Control your apps or they'll control you

Check the Facebook apps you use to see whether they can access your information (i.e., your complete profile and activities as well as some of the information of your friends), track your location and post status updates and photos on your behalf.

You can block specific apps at the Facebook App Settings page.

You can also turn off apps connected to your account on the App Settings page by clicking Edits (to the right of "Apps you use") and then clicking Turn Off Platform.

Make sure you also deal with apps that others use so that you can control your information given to app developers on apps your Friends install.

You'll also want to turn off "Instant personalization" to prevent Facebook from sharing your information with certain third-party sites.

Some third-party apps can access your list of Facebook Friends.

You may decide to delete apps but the horse may have already left the barn if the app already has information on you.

Control your friends' apps

If you want to prevent friends from sending your information to their Facebook apps, select "Apps others use," click Edit and uncheck information you don't want shared. Then click to save your changes.

Your payment information

Since any website can be hacked, you don't want to unnecessarily have your credit-card information floating out there. Even though Facebook wants to know your credit-card information in case you make purchases through the website, you don't have to provide this information to Facebook. If you won't be making these types of purchases, then change the Account Settings so this information is removed.

Deactivating your Facebook account

With deactivation, your profile is removed from the site as well as most of your postings (however, certain items will still be there). Your data is still with Facebook and you can reactivate your account at a later date.

Deleting your Facebook account

If you delete your account, it's gone. If you later want to be on Facebook, you'll have to set up a new account. So before you delete an account, download a copy of all of the data you've published.

*****

Google

The Google "free lunch"

Google offers free email, search, maps, photo software, web browsing, cloud storage and more but there's no free Google lunch. The payment Google wants for these services is not cash but instead information about you. As time goes by and more of your information is stored and analyzed by Google, you become more valuable to Google and the true cost of your free lunch goes up.

Of course, the "free lunch" concept does not apply only to Google. It also affects any company where you "volunteer" your data in return for free stuff.

Google keeps track of every search you do as well as the Gmails you send and receive, the YouTube videos you watch and your location if you use Google Maps.

Go to the Google MyAccount page at: https://myaccount.google.com/intro to have better control of personal information, privacy and security.

Benefits of diversification

As noted earlier, one way to protect your information is to use more than one company for different services—don't have email, calendar, Internet searches, digital assistants, TV, messaging and phone with just one company. Diversification helps prevent accumulation of your information in one place (e.g., with Google).

Another benefit of diversification is the information you see when you search. For example, Google filters search results based on your prior searches so the results can be skewed to show you just what Google thinks you want to see based on your past searches, which isn't necessarily what you want to see today.

Benefits of signing out of Google

If you stay signed into Google (whether it's your Gmail account, YouTube, etc.), you are giving Google additional opportunities to track your location and accumulate more information on you.

Google Authenticator and two-factor authentication (2FA)

One of the best ways to protect your security is to use Google Authenticator with its two-factor authentication to verify your identity on your devices. Besides requiring a special code in addition to your password to access a Google service, you can get alerts if inappropriate access is attempted.

Go to https://myaccount.google.com/ to set this up. Then any time you or anyone else logs into Google on an unfamiliar computer, tablet, cellphone or browser, a code will need to be entered to get access. You can decide whether to get future codes via text, a phone call or Google's Authenticator app.

You can also set it up so you get notification if someone else is trying to log into your account.

When you lose, trade in, donate or have a device stolen, be sure to remove the device from your Google account.

Passwords

Have a strong, unique, complex password and change it at least every six months. It's not a good idea to reuse your passwords at multiple places, especially your Google password.

If you're using the Google Chrome Internet browser, there is a Password Alert add-on (extension) that helps prevent you from entering your Google password on other sites. This can help you if a website is posing as another website. The extension is available from the Chrome Web Store.

Google security

Go to the security settings page for your Google account and adjust the settings on:

Recovery information
Recent activity
Account permissions
App passwords
Two-Factor Authentication (called 2-Step Verification here)

Google privacy settings

The Google website privacy.google.com answers many of your questions about privacy and security with Google products and how to take actions using Google's My Account feature to:

- Turn off features such as location tracking and ads tied to your search queries, viewed YouTube videos or visits to websites

- Direct you to the Google page where prior visits to websites can be deleted

Gmail

You can take steps to make your Gmail account more secure.

- Do an account Security Checkup.

  Go to the Security Checkup section of My Account page at https://myaccount.google.com/intro?pli=1

- Update your account recovery options.

- Have a unique, strong, complex password and don't use it on any other website.

- Protect your password—don't leave it by your computer, send it by email or give it to anyone.

- Never enter your password after following a link in an email from an untrusted site. Always go mail.google.com

- Enroll in 2-step verification.

  2-step verification adds an extra layer of security to your account by requiring you to sign in with something you know (your password) and something you have in hand (a code sent to your phone).

- Take a look at Google's privacy policy. You are giving Google a "worldwide license to use…communicate, publish,…, and distribute such content" even after you stop using Google services.

Google (Android) phones

If you want to get Android security updates as soon as possible for your phone, get a Google Nexus phone. Other manufacturers using Android don't issue security updates as quickly as Google.

Protecting the privacy of your Google searches

You have a few choices for protecting the privacy of your Internet searches.

First, you could use one browser for searches and another one for everything else. Second, if you want to use a search engine that doesn't track you, consider DuckDuckGo. It may be available as an extension (or option) on your browser.

How to download all of your Google search history

Go to https://history.google.com/history (sign into your Google account) and you can get a copy of your Google search history by clicking Download on the Settings menu. Don't do this on a public computer such as at a library.

Deleting your search history

To see how to delete Google searches and a history of websites you visited, go to
https://support.google.com/websearch/answer/465?hl=en

You can either delete individual searches or your entire search history. Even if you delete your search history, that won't prevent future searches from being recorded unless you turn off your Web history in its entirety.

Google still has all of your search history but by invoking this option, your history won't be used to target ads to you or customize your search results based on your searching history. To stop all targeted ads, opt out at the Google Ads Settings page.

You can also delete searches and sites stored in your browser (e.g., Chrome, Safari, Internet Explorer, Edge and Firefox) or the Google Toolbar.

Preventing future searches from being saved

You can do this on the Web and Activity page by enabling "Pause History."

Google location

If you have an Android device, Google keeps track of your location and maps it with timestamps and animation.

You can turn off the entire location history on Google's

servers by going to https://support.google.com/gmm/answer/3118687?hl=en and turning Location History off and deleting part or all of your Location History.

Location History is also used by Google Wallet or Now. You can turn it off for all purposes.

It's one thing to turn Google location off. That doesn't delete your location history unless you go to the Location history page, choose Location Reporting, clicking "Do not report" to turn it off and then delete some or all of the entries.

To disable Google's location reporting on an iPhone, disable Location Reporting on the Google search app, Google+ and other Google apps on your phone. To see all the apps tracking your location on your phone, go to Settings, then Privacy and finally to Location Services. Similarly, for Android phones, go to Settings, then Location, then Google Location Reporting and turn it off.

Google Maps now includes a "Your Timeline" feature that shows your entire location history on Google Maps. It's based on data from your devices when you're signed into your Google account. This information is also found in your Google My Account dashboard.

Stopping Shared Endorsements

Just like Facebook, Google's privacy policy defaults to your giving permission for you and your photo (as it is on Google+) to appear in ads. With Google's Shared Endorsements, when you rate something it can show up in search results with your name and photo. You can opt out of Shared Endorsements.

How to Google yourself

Since a blind date, significant other, current or future employer may Google you, do you know what they'll see?

- If not, then consider putting your name in a Google search and see the results. You *may* also want to search on your social-networking usernames, too. Before taking these steps, think about whether you're providing more information for Google by doing these searches.

- While you're at it, you can see what photos are out there on you in Google Images. Besides searching for your name, you can search for an image of yourself. Just click the camera button in the search bar and drag or upload an image (unless you think this will cause more trouble than it's worth).

How to get alerts about you

To know when you pop up online, you can set up a Google Alert at: https://www.google.com/alerts

Deleting your Google account

If you decide to delete your account, you'll first want to back up your information.

Google Voice

You may need a way to keep your phone numbers private and to screen phone calls. With Google Voice, you can give out a Google phone number rather than your cell, home or business number. Calls are forwarded from the Google number to the phone number you designate and your privacy is maintained.

YouTube

Google's YouTube likes to keep track of what you're watching. You can either delete all of your viewing history or selectively delete your history.

To prevent future tracking of your habits, you can permanently stop recording your viewing history by pausing your watch history.

Android

Android is the Google operating system for computers, tablets, smartphones and more. Unlike the closed Apple operating system, Android is a product that can be modified by manufacturers and others, which means, in general, there may be more security concerns with Android products. Be more careful with Android apps.

*****

Microsoft

Scammers posing as Microsoft

A very common scam is for someone to call you and say they are from Microsoft calling about unusual activity on your computer that can be fixed for a fee. These calls are scams. Microsoft will not call you. If you get this type of call, just hang up.

Windows 10

First off, be on the lookout for scammers' emails telling you to update to Windows 10 and providing a place for you to click.

Even if you do update to Windows 10 from a legitimate Microsoft source, be aware that you may be giving Microsoft more access to your information than you realize.

You can use the easy or custom Windows 10 installation. The easy installation provides fewer privacy protections for you. The custom installation is more protective because it allows you to turn off Wi-Fi sharing, location tracking and collection of your information by advertisers.

You can set up either a local account or a cloud account. A local account on your device shares less information with Microsoft but doesn't allow you to use cloud features.

You'll want to look at the account privacy settings for contacts, location, calendar and more.

During the setup of Windows 10, if you agree to sync (link) your Microsoft 10 user account to your Microsoft account, Microsoft will be backing up your browsing history, passwords and more. You can turn syncing off.

Automatic update alert

Be aware that in 2016 Windows 10 will become a "Recommended Update" for users of prior versions of Windows. This means that if you have automatic updates set up to be installed on your device, it will automatically upload Windows 10 and start its installer. You may want to allow automatic updates but manually control the installation of the updates so you can bypass installing Windows 10.

Microsoft Privacy Settings

Microsoft's Window 10 uses the same operating system across all devices (i.e., computers, tablets and smartphones). There is a way to control privacy and specify which apps and services will be able to access different data. To see and set these controls, go to https://account.microsoft.com/privacy/about

Cortana personal assistant

You need to decide whether to allow Microsoft's personal assistant, Cortana, to learn about your browsing, calendar, contacts, location, and more.

Microsoft privacy statement

Regarding Microsoft's privacy statement, the European digital rights organization (EDRi) says: "Microsoft basically grants itself very broad rights to collect everything you do, say and write with and on your devices in order to sell more targeted advertising or to sell your data to third parties."

Microsoft is not unusual in what it collects on customers but to its credit it is pretty up front about what it collects.

As of the time this book is being written, according to Microsoft's privacy statement, the data Microsoft collects may include your name; email address; postal address; phone number; passwords; password hints; your age; gender; country; preferred language; data about your interests and favorites; credit-card numbers; Web pages you visit; search terms you enter; your devices and networks; your contacts; your location; the content of your documents, photos, music and videos you upload; and the content of your communications sent or received.

For more info, see https://www.microsoft.com/en-us/privacystatement/

Windows XP

Microsoft no longer supports Windows XP with security and other software updates. Even though the antivirus product you use may continue supporting Windows XP, you'll probably want to upgrade to a more current, supported version of Windows if you want to continue using the Microsoft operating system.

Microsoft Office

Check whether your older version of Microsoft Office still gets security updates.

*****

Social-Networking Sites and Apps

Much of what was discussed above in this chapter applies whether you're using Facebook, Instagram, Periscope, Pinterest, Snapchat, Twitter or other social-networking sites, apps or games (including Pokémon Go). Be careful when using and/or posting on these and other social-networking sites and make sure the privacy settings on these sites meet your needs.

For example, with Pokémon Go, the game needs GPS (and your location) to work. You may want to use more discretion in selecting areas in which to play the game if you know your location is being recorded. Similarly, if you take pictures while playing the game, you could be revealing where you took the photo if location tracking is on. Even think about how you sign up for the game. If you use your usual email account (e.g., Gmail), your Pokémon Go activity will be linked up to your personal information—at some point, that information may be available to other players. Finally, pick a unique screen name that can't be linked up to your other social-networking sites.

Don't overshare on social-networking sites. If you post too much information about yourself, an identity thief can find information about your life, use it to answer security or "challenge" questions on your personal, medical and financial accounts and get access to your data and money. Consider limiting access to your networking page to a small group of people. Never post your full name, Social Security number, home or work address, phone number or account numbers in publicly accessible sites. Otherwise, you may also be putting your personal safety in jeopardy.

Even if you delete a post on your end, it still may reside on the recipient's device. If you're told that what you post will disappear on the recipient's device, it still may be on the server of the website, app or third parties that have access to it.

See if your employer prohibits employees from using their work email address on social-networking sites.

Other protective steps to take

- Read the privacy and security policies before you sign up for apps and at websites so you have at least some idea where your information may end up. See if you're granting a worldwide, perpetual, royalty-free license for the site to store, use, edit and publish your content in any form or share it with advertisers or business partners.

- Minimize the personal and other information you provide during registration.

- See if you can register without using your actual name.

- Think more than twice during the registration process if you're asked to provide your email password to allow the social network access to your email address book.

- Use strong, complex passwords and use unique passwords for each social-networking site.

- Use a special email address just for social-networking sites.

- Screen friend requests.

- Be wary of emails asking you to update your online profile.

- Assume everything you post on the Internet will be there forever. There are websites that archive old postings and websites. Don't post anything you wouldn't want a current or future school, employer or significant other to see.

- Before downloading files, see what the extension is (e.g., an ".exe" file may contain malware) by unblocking hidden file extensions.

- If you're unsure about the safety of taking a step, don't do it.

- With more hackers getting access to email and bank accounts, social-engineering fraud-insurance coverage is becoming more common to help pay for losses.

- See whether your photos are really public (even if you've set your privacy setting to private) because you shared at the same time with another social-networking site or app.

- See if you simultaneously share the link to your photos with other networks, whether not only your followers but *anyone* can see the photos.

Twitter

Your tweets may live forever, even if you delete them. The Library of Congress is in the process of acquiring Twitter's entire archive of tweets and planning to make it all available to researchers.

Have a strong, unique password for your Twitter account.

If you decide to delete a Twitter account, first back up your tweets. Note that after deleting your account, much of your information may still show up in search-engine results.

Index

56795843R00126

Made in the USA
San Bernardino, CA
14 November 2017